Strategic Living

Strategic Living

How to Set and Accomplish
Life-Changing Goals

Don J. McMinn

BAKER BOOK HOUSE
Grand Rapids, Michigan 49516

ISBN: 0-8010-6241-1

Printed in the United States of America

Contents

Introduction

o you remember the incident in *Alice in Wonderland* where Alice is talking to the Cheshire cat who is perched up in a tree? Alice is a bit confused about her direction. She asks the cat, "Would you tell me, please, which way I ought to go from here?" "That depends a great deal on where you want to go," replies the Cheshire cat. "I don't much care where," says Alice. To which the feline replies, "Then it doesn't matter which way you go."

There are many people who, like Alice, have no direction in life. Like the ball in a pinball machine, they bounce around and react to different situations until they finally run out of energy, and then they drop out of sight. Life is just a series of knee-jerk reactions to emotional whims and circumstances. And, like a ship with a broken rudder, these people drift aimlessly through life, at the mercy of changing currents and high winds. However, I remind you—you never drift any place worth going.

Fortunately, you don't *have* to drift through life. You

can chart a course, hoist the sails, and channel your efforts toward desired results. And that's what strategic living is all about—gaining control of your life and your future. Strategic living is a planned, systematic approach to optimizing your resources. It involves planning, not as an attempt to foretell the future; rather as a way to regulate and shape the future by controlling present action.

Edward de Bono says (de Bono 1984, 143), "Strategy means putting things in place carefully, and with a great deal of thought. It is the opposite of just waiting for things to happen or taking a flyer." For a builder, a strategy can be a set of architectural drawings. For a coach, it can be a simple game plan. A teacher's strategy would include the development of a curriculum and lesson plans.

I'm going to talk about strategy as it relates to *your personal life*. The focus of this book is on *you*—your talents, your resources, your time, your future. Perhaps you think strategy is only for executives and generals, and inappropriate for personal use. A quick check of your planning "vital signs" may develop more receptivity to the idea. Answer the following questions and consider their implications.

1. Are you where you are today because you planned to get there, or are you there because that's where you got beached?
2. Do you have any written plans?
3. Do you have anything in the near and distant future to look forward to?
4. Are you maximizing your potential?
5. Are you steadily improving in all these areas: educational, financial, professional, family, spiritual, personal?
6. In general, are you progressing, stagnant, or regressing?

If these vital signs are anemic, you need to get serious about personal planning. Most people fail in life not because of a lack of ability, intellect, or opportunity; they've just never organized their energies around a central goal. Avoid the Alice-in-Wonderland approach to life—make a commitment to conscientious strategic planning.

1

Why Bother?
Nine Reasons Why Life Planning/Goal Setting Is Important

t's finally my turn. I am summoned to appear before the high court of heaven. The interrogation begins.

> *Don McMinn—Born and raised in optimum conditions: loving, Christian parents, an American citizen in the twentieth century, unrestrictive educational opportunities, many friends, lots of opportunities— much should be required of this man because he was given much. Give an account of yourself.*

You were given a measure of musical talent. Was that ever developed or was it neglected?

You were blessed with financial resources. Report on your stewardship.

In your lifetime you had hundreds of close friends and acquaintances. How did you influence them?

In your early years you had a problem with impatience. Did you ever overcome that sin?

Why were you overweight?

What kind of father and husband were you?

Were you as good in your profession as you could have been?

The last ten years of your life—were they productive years?

You were given specific spiritual gifts. Were they exercised?

You were commanded to love and show mercy. Did you?

The questioning continues. I am made acutely aware that during my life God entrusted me with many assets for which I am now accountable. My stewardship is being examined.

My interpretation of this future event may be open to discussion and examination, but the fact that it's going to happen is not.

For we shall all stand before the judgment seat of God. . . .
So then each one of us shall give account of himself to God (Rom. 14:10, 12).

We need to get serious about life. We need to get serious about being good trustees of what God has given us. We need to get serious about the productivity of our lives—because God is serious about it.

Do you remember the parable of the talents (Matt. 25)? A man, about to go on a journey, gave three of his servants different amounts of assets, *according to their abilities*. One was given five talents, another two talents, and another one talent. When the master returned he required his servants to report on their stewardship. The one who had been given five talents gained five more. The one with two talents also doubled his assets. To these men the master said, "Well done, good and faithful slave; you were faithful with a few things, I will put you in charge of many things; enter into the joy of your master" (v. 23). But the slave with one talent, being afraid of losing what he had, hid his talent in the ground. When his master returned, one talent was all the slave had. He was rebuked with these words: "You wicked, lazy slave; you knew that I reap where I did not sow, and gather where I scattered no *seed*. Then you ought to have put my money in the bank, and on my arrival I would have received my *money* back with interest. Therefore take away the talent from him, and give it to the one who has the ten talents" (vv. 26–28).

Why did Jesus tell this parable? What is he teaching? The lesson is fourfold: God expects us to be good stewards of all he has given us; there will be a day of accounting; we will be judged based upon what we did with what we were given, not on the final balance (the two faithful men received the same reward); and, we will be rewarded or punished according to our degree of faithfulness.

God is serious about the productivity of our lives. Are we?

A recent survey revealed that only 5 percent of Americans write down personal goals. I'm sure many have goals in their mind, but my experience convinces me that only those who write down goals are serious about achievement. It's like going on a diet but not telling anyone—it's too easy to cheat. The 95 percent who don't write down goals are shortchanging themselves. Among Christian people this fact has great bearing on the kingdom of God and its progress around the world. It's no wonder we're

losing ground in our attempt to influence the world with
the gospel. Most of God's people are at half-throttle.

I'm going to give you nine reasons why life
planning/goal setting (the essence of *strategic living*) is
important. This is my attempt to convert you. If you're
not convinced that your life will be enhanced by planning
and goal setting, you'll not participate. You must be convinced that it's worth the effort. Hear me out!

**First, life planning/goal setting helps us to reach
our maximum potential in life and leads us to
the "abundant life" which Christ promised in
John 10:10.**

If during our lifetime we follow our plans without con-
sulting God as to his plan for our lives, we will inevitably
live less than fulfilling lives. Regardless of what great
plans you may have for your life, God's plans are greater.
If you want to accomplish ten major objectives in your
lifetime, he probably has twelve or fifteen to challenge
you with. Some think that God's will is restrictive and,
like the tiny shoes some Oriental women wear, it will
stunt our growth and potential. Not so!

Let God Set the Boundaries

Consider the teaching of Ephesians 3:20, "Now to Him
who is able to do exceeding abundantly beyond all that
we ask or think, according to the power that works within
us." We must allow God to set the boundaries of our potential. He made us and he knows us better than we know
ourselves. If we lean on our own understanding, our plans
will always leave us root-bound. Only by committing ourselves to the divine plan can we live life to its fullest.

I'm not just referring to spiritual aspects, although
they are the most important. Even in regard to our fi-

nances, education, professional status and other areas of life, the way of blessing is the way of his will. God's plan for our lives will always be greater than our plans.

This is the testimony of Gideon as recorded in Judges 6. When we first meet Gideon, he's beating out wheat (a rather menial task), and he's doing it on the floor of a winepress. Every farmer knows you shouldn't beat wheat inside a winepress because there's no breeze to blow the chaff away. But Gideon is afraid the Midianites are going to steal his wheat, so he's doing it the hard way. An angel of the Lord appears and addresses him as a "valiant warrior." Has the angel gotten his instructions confused? He must have stopped at the wrong winepress, for it becomes obvious from reading the rest of the chapter that Gideon was anything *but* a valiant warrior. He was a pessimist and a coward. When told that he would be Israel's deliverer, he immediately began to give excuses: "Behold, my family is the least in Manasseh, and I am the youngest in my father's house" (v. 15). He asked for two different confirmations of the Lord's instructions (vv. 17–21 and 36–40), and he was so afraid of his father's household and the men of the city that his first mission was conducted at night.

Why, then, did the Lord call him a *valiant warrior*? Because God saw in Gideon what he would one day become, and not what he was, standing on the floor of the winepress. The turning point was when the "Spirit of the LORD came upon Gideon." From then on, Gideon stepped into the realm of the "exceeding abundantly."

Gideon eventually led a reduced army of 300 men against an enemy that numbered 135,000 and came forth victorious! If Gideon had been content with setting his own boundaries, he would have spent most of his years beating wheat. If he had listened to the opinion of his family and friends, his fate would have been the same.

Instead, he listened to the voice of God and became more than he would have ever asked or thought.

It has been said, "Man can count the number of seeds in an apple, but only God can count the number of apples in a seed." We see ourselves as apples—fruit with limited potential. But God sees us as seeds with unlimited potential for fruit. We look at ourselves and others and, with our limited vision and insight, we "size everyone up" and put them in a box. Even our self-esteem is usually determined by the opinions of others. A bad self-image is developed by listening to what others think about us, whereas a good self-image is developed by hearing God's opinion. Likewise a limited life vision is developed by listening to what others think is our potential; a maximum life vision is developed by accepting what God has established as our potential.

The Half-a-Tank Syndrome

I'm convinced that most people will die only half "used up"; they will leave this world with half-a-tank of gas left. Why do most people put their minds into neutral soon after their formal education is finished? We inevitably find ourselves in a position of stalemate midway through life. The years go by without any new skill development, intellectual curiosity, spiritual maturity, or for that matter, any significant progress. The epitaph of many Americans will sadly read: DIED, AGE 25, BURIED, AGE 75.

Even our social-welfare system encourages early withdrawal from the progress lane. Our social security system prepares us to "retire" at age sixty-five, and even to slow down as that magic age draws near. We have deprived our country of its most capable leaders. Men and women through the ages have reached their prime in their sixties and seventies, but we mentally prepare our elders to go fishing. Do you remember Arthur Rubinstein, who in his nineties, hobbled across a concert stage, sat down at a grand piano and played a Mozart Piano Concerto with a major symphony orchestra. Thousands of notes played with artistic interpretation—all from memory. I'm glad someone didn't suggest to Rubenstein that he had to retire at sixty-five!

And what about those "ruts" we fall into? (Someone has defined a *rut* as "a grave with both ends knocked out.") Ruts dispense a steady flow of anesthetic that inhibits achievement. And the longer you stay in a rut, the deeper it gets. Even if our occupation puts us in a rut because it only requires nonthinking, rote work, that's no reason why our lives should take on such a posture. The remaining hours of the day can be filled with directed, purposeful events. It's so easy to slip into the nonprogress mode and so very hard to get out.

No Arbitrary Standard

Of course it's important to realize that everyone has his/her own capacity. By *capacity* I mean the speed with which a person functions, the amount he can negotiate at one time, and the total amount he can eventually handle. Everyone's aptitude is different. Some people can juggle more balls than others—we all have our limits. There is danger in comparing ourselves with others and comparing other people with some arbitrary standard. If I try to keep stride with someone who has more capacity, I'll become frustrated and eventually exhausted. And if I pace myself with those who have a lower saturation level, I'll become an underachiever (though I cannot accuse them of underachievement). One individual may be able to work fulltime, take eight hours of college classwork, raise two

children, and take a cross-stitching class on Saturdays—
and be able to do all of it well. The same schedule may
drive another person insane. We need to establish a com-
fortable yet challenging pace which is right for us; one
which will prevent burnout but likewise guard against
being left with half-a-tank of gas. In the last speech he
made, Will Rogers said, "Lord, let me live until I'm dead."

What is the antidote for underachievement? How *do*
we get out of ruts? How *do* we discover the number of
apples in a seed? What *is* our capacity? Life planning/goal
setting helps us deal with these issues.

Strategic living is active, progressive living. It allows
for a good assessment of where we are, but then points
us toward a challenging future. It motivates us to be all
that God wants us to be. It maximizes God's investment
in our lives. Strategic living will not find us sitting in
front of the TV very often, nor will it allow us to waste
our finances on nonbudget items. It will not tolerate laziness and frowns on wasted time and energy. In short,
strategic living makes us effective and efficient.

Live Abundantly

Life planning/goal setting also helps us to experience
the "abundant life" that Christ promised in John 10:10.
"I came that they might have life, and might have it
abundantly." This Scripture often seems to be an elusive
promise that is beyond the reach of most Christians. But
if it's the reason for which he came, then it's meant for
all Christians, *all* of the time. Why is it then that most
Christians are not experiencing life abundant? They have
life, but they have not tapped into the added adjective—
abundant.

The Greek word for "abundant" is *perisseuo,* which
means "to superabound in quantity and to be superior in

quality, to be beyond measure, to be exceedingly abundantly above." It is the same word used in the Ephesians 3:20 passage we just discussed. ("*Now to Him who is able to do exceeding* abundantly . . ."). Christ is not just talking about life, but quality of life. He's stating that Christians can experience a quality of life that would otherwise be impossible without the presence of God. There are many highly successful lost people who set and reach goals, achieve great results, attain high standards of accomplishment, and are admired by many. But Christ offers the Christian more than that; it's a new dimension. I'm convinced that part of the abundance comes from *knowing that I am currently fulfilling God's design for my life and that my life, though in a small way, is contributing to his master plan for the universe.* Abundant living is *purposeful* living. Abundant living is knowing that you're in sync with the divine plan.

Several years ago my wife and I were experiencing the difficulties of being a one-car family. I sought the Lord relative to purchasing another car and he led me to a 1975 Datsun B210 that had 97,000 miles on the odometer. It certainly wasn't what I had in mind, but the moment I saw the car I knew it was God's provision for us. I had owned nicer and more impressive automobiles in my life, but I was convinced that God wanted me to drive that old Datsun. It's hard to explain, but for as long as I drove the car (five years) I had a deep sense of satisfaction because I knew he wanted me to drive that particular car. In this area of my life, I experienced abundant living. Who would think that driving an old car could bring peace and contentment? I could have purchased another newer auto, but it would not have been the same; the "abundant" factor would not have been there.

Likewise, I am blessed to have an "abundant marriage." There are 3 billion women on planet Earth, but

only Mary Craig McMinn was fashioned for me and me
for her. Though the odds of finding her were not good—
I did, and I'm glad.

In short, I'm living the abundant life because I'm married to the right woman, working at the right job, driving
the right car, living in the right house—I'm in the center
of his will and that's where life is abundant! We seldom
stumble into God's will; we must seek and discover it. It's
not hard to find, but you do have to look and life plan-
ning/goal setting helps us look. It involves systematically
searching for God's will and then doing it.

Second, life planning/goal setting helps us to focus all our resources toward meaningful projects.

In a football game, the offensive unit has one goal in
mind—to transport an oddly shaped, inflated pigskin
across an arbitrarily drawn chalkline. Think about it—
all available resources are focused toward that one goal.
The quarterback offers his agility and strong arm, the
tailback tenders his speed and maneuverability, and the
guard contributes his strength. All eleven men channel
their physical abilities, skills, experience, and motivation
toward one goal. Additionally, the coach on the sideline,
the offensive coordinator in the press box, the alumni
club, the scouting team, the recruiting group, every facet
of the entire organization is committed to the achievement of that one goal. But without a common goal, those
resources would be wasted, they would remain unfocused
and undirected. A shared goal is what ties all the various
parts of a football team together.

A goal will have the same effect in our personal lives
as it does on a group of athletes. A goal will help unify,
focus, and direct resources. Even dormant and unknown
resources become activated by a goal. Strategic living pro-

vides for the accurate assessment of individual resources and then ensures that these assets work together for the accomplishment of meaningful goals.

A typical concern expressed by many people is: "I don't have much to work with, I'm very limited in resources." Let them stand corrected—we all have more resources than we know what to do with. Few people ever take the time to accurately assess their resources, but nevertheless, they are there. Let me suggest a few.

Time

Do you realize how much time you have, and how little time it takes to perform meaningful activities? In a period of five minutes you can: call a friend, read your child a story, take a shower, memorize a Scripture, write a letter, jog one-half mile, read a psalm, order flowers for your wife or husband, peel an orange and eat it, make arrangements for a special evening, feed and pet your dog, the list is endless!

Calculating sixteen waking hours per day, you could perform 192 five-minute functions every day. Our problem is not a lack of time, we just don't know what to do with the time we have. You have as many hours in your day as King David did, as many as the president of the United States, and as many as Jesus had when he was incarnate on the earth. What have you accomplished in the past three years? Jesus performed his entire earthly ministry in that time span. Yes, time is a valuable resource, and God has given to each man equally.

Gifts, Talents, Skills

The day you received Christ as your Savior, the Holy Spirit endowed you with at least one *spiritual gift,* prob-

ably more. Do you know what your gift is? You might
have a supernatural ability to teach (gift of teaching),
you could be very adept at making and managing money
(gift of giving), or you could discover that you have a
great proclivity toward organization and administration
(gift of leading). Your spiritual gift could potentially be
your greatest asset. (See Romans 12 and 1 Corinthians 12
for more information on gifts.)

Whereas *gifts* are supernatural abilities given at spiritual birth, *talents* are natural abilities given at physical
birth. One may have a talent in music, an unusually good
athletic ability, or a talent in communicating with people.
I believe everyone is talented in one or more areas, though
sometimes a talent may be undiscovered. I have a friend
who is talented musically but didn't know it until he was
twenty-five years old because he had never sat down to
play the piano. What are your talents?

Skills are abilities which you work to acquire. One
may have developed the ability to type, sew, play tennis,
use a computer, or speak Spanish. A skill is not something
you're "endowed" with; it's simply something you work to
acquire. You can choose to develop a skill just like you
choose an entrée at a cafeteria.

Personal Influence, Friends, and Family

Everyone has a sphere of influence that they both affect and from which they can draw resources. Your sphere
of influence includes family, neighbors, friends, acquaintances, business associates, and others. And they repre-
sent a vast reservoir of resources. For instance, a well-
respected dentist used his influence among his colleagues
to staff a medical-mission trip. A housewife drew upon
her influence among neighborhood friends to begin a baby-
sitting club. A business executive called upon a former

employee to design some computer software for his new firm. Consider the time, gifts, talents, and skills of all the people you know. Add all these factors together, and you'll discover a tremendous reservoir of resources.

Have you ever considered the limitless resources of a local body of believers? Suppose a church has four hundred active members. Think of all the business associates, friends, neighbors, relatives, and school acquaintances these four hundred members have. All of these people can be affected by the church, and to some degree the church can draw upon them to reach its objectives.

I've listed a few resources everyone has, a personalized list would include many more. Once resources are identified, the question is: are they being channeled in the proper direction? Are they working in consonance toward a well-thought-out goal or are they drifting aimlessly, often interfering with one another? There is an enormous amount of momentum that can be generated when all that we are, have, and have access to, is pointed in one direction. The singular goal of "I want to be a medical doctor" can trigger all sorts of resources—the next ten years of your life, financial resources from family members, recommendations to get accepted into medical school from an influential uncle, prior education (B.S.) as a prerequisite to med school, and the list goes on and on.

A goal has a magnetic effect on resources. It's like a raft that is drifting aimlessly in the ocean. There are five men on board the raft, all in good physical condition, but they're not paddling because they don't know which way to go—they're aimless. They remain dormant and the currents arbitrarily determine their direction. Suddenly one of the men spots an island on the horizon, and there quickly develops among them a common desire: get to the island as quickly as possible. All resources are now channeled toward a common goal; all five men use their physical and mental faculties to move their raft toward the island.

This is what strategic living does for our personal lives. It helps us to set meaningful goals, and then it identifies and organizes all of our resources toward the achievement of these goals. The result is a life marked by purpose, drive, effectiveness, and efficiency.

Third, life planning/goal setting promotes and preserves unity and harmony.

Amos 3:3 asks, "Can two walk together, except they be agreed?" (KJV). The implied answer is, "Very difficult if not impossible." It's hard for two people to function in harmony if they're not in agreement as to where they're going and why and how they want to get there.

Walking Together

During a planning conference I once asked members of a church staff to write down the purpose for which their church existed. I received as many different answers as there were people present. There was no unanimity in their minds as to why their enterprise existed. This disparateness had an acute bearing on their effectiveness as a church. There was no consensus on where they were going, so it was hard to achieve unity and harmony.

Many couples experience trauma in their marriage because they fail to see the importance of Amos 3:3. Their children are social pests because they never "agreed" on a policy of discipline; one was a loose disciplinarian while the other was stringent. Some families are in a financial mess because they've never decided how they're going to "walk together" relative to the handling of finances. And some spouses are totally unaware of the deep, long-term desires of their partner and therefore can provide little support toward the fulfillment of these visions.

Many businesses also suffer from this lack of common direction. Perhaps at one time the goals and plans of the business were crystal clear and well communicated to all employees. But through the years, due to changes in management, growth in the size of the business, a shift in the climate of the market, and other factors—those goals and plans which were once distinct and understandable became ambiguous, providing little if any harmony and motivation.

Every three months my staff and I write out plans and goals for the next quarter. We also spend time evaluating the previous quarter. By the time the planning/evaluation process is complete (which may take a week or two), there is a great sense of unanimity as to where we're going and how we're going to get there. It allows us to join hands and "walk together."

My wife is always informed of my plans and goals; there are few surprises. There are no unexpected purchases around our house because we operate on a budget and all nonbudgeted expenses are discussed at length. We have agreed on our approach to childrearing and discipline; therefore there is peace and harmony in this area. Several years ago a popular phrase stated that "families that pray together, stay together." Anyone who has experienced family life for more than a few years realizes that while this formula may be true, it's not complete. Families that want to stay together must—among other things—work, play, talk, and worship together. I would suggest another requirement: "Families that *plan* together, stay together, and do so more harmoniously."

Another important aspect in establishing unity through goal setting is that those who will be an integral part of the fulfillment of the plans should be involved in their formulation. If both the husband and wife are going to live within the restraints of a budget, then both should be involved in its conception. If a family vacation is being considered, everyone involved should be given the opportunity for input. There is great truth in the old management adage, "People support what they help to create." When plans are "handed down" from above, they are often received with apathy, but when plans are generated "from within," they are enthusiastically supported.

There is also value in sharing our goals and plans with those who will, in any way, be affected by the execution of the plans. Not only will they be more understanding of our lives, but they will often be an encouragement or even a direct help in the accomplishment of our plans. In the process of communicating our plans, we will inevitably receive valuable feedback which will help to refine and clarify the plans. Clearly defined goals and plans provide the basic building blocks of harmony and unity among any group of people whether it be a family, church, business, or social club.

Becoming "Single-minded"

Plans and goals not only contribute to unity within a group of people, but they will also help establish unity within an individual. When someone conscientiously works through the planning process, he will inevitably become single-minded; a distinct sense of unity and harmony will be apparent in his life.

James 1:8 says, "A double-minded man [is] unstable in all his ways." A double-minded man is one who is constantly fluctuating between several diverse alternatives. One day he is moving full throttle toward one concern; the next day he is pursuing an interest in the opposite direction. As a result, nothing significant is ever accomplished. Even more problematic is the fact that the Bible says that a double-minded man is unstable in *all* his ways; it affects every area of his life. If a man is double-minded in regard to his occupation, it will also affect his marriage and relationship with his children. The repercussions of being double-minded ripple through all areas of life.

On the contrary, a single-minded man is a joy to observe. He is a man of direction who is not easily diverted by distractions. He is a man of convictions who is not easily persuaded to stray outside the boundaries of his beliefs. He is a man of accomplishment because he is focused. A single-minded man is stable in all his ways, there is a consistency and settledness to his lifestyle. He's the type of person you want on your side because his commitments are firm.

How do we become single-minded? The answer is more complex than the simple solution that I offer, but I'm convinced that careful and thorough planning will help develop and solidify single-mindedness in our lives. When we plan, there is a certain mental process that we go through that cultivates single-mindedness. In the planning process, we realize that we must choose between many options and commit to a few. This process of voluntary elimination develops a level of commitment which is otherwise not possible.

The establishment of harmony and unity is a good by-product of the planning process. In the midst of a social environment that seems to spawn instability and diversity, God would have us be people of stability and permanence. Life planning will help us achieve this posture.

Fourth, life planning/goal setting helps us live productive lives.

There seems to be a law in the universe which says, "Good requires effort, bad requires nothing." In other words, doing good is like paddling upstream—it takes effort. If you put your oars in the boat you'll start going downstream.

Improvement and advancement always requires conscientious action. If you're satisfied to be illiterate and uneducated, you don't have to do anything, but it takes effort to become educated. It's not hard to be poor, but it takes conscientious action to produce income. Likewise, a good marriage doesn't just "happen," it takes effort: planned, intelligent effort. And children don't just "turn out good," their natural inclination is bent toward the negative so they must be taught and disciplined. For instance, most children are not, by nature, neat and orderly. These character traits must be developed.

This law is true also in the spiritual realm. It takes no effort to live in the flesh and to be backslidden, but it takes effort to be filled with the Spirit and to grow in the Lord. Spiritual disciplines such as reading the Bible, praying, witnessing, and going to church are not in the natural flow of our inclinations.

John Gardner, author of *Excellence* (Gardner 1961, 109–110) puts it this way:

> Some people may have greatness thrust upon them. Very few have excellence thrust upon them. They achieve it. They do not achieve it unwittingly, by 'doing what comes naturally'; and they don't stumble into it in the course of amusing themselves. All excellence involves discipline and tenacity of purpose.

This is why goal setting is so important. Good things in life require effort to achieve, but effort is a useless commodity unless it is channeled toward a purpose. If we want to live productive lives we have to know where we're going and then put our oars in the water and row.

Fifth, life planning/goal setting helps us maintain a constant, sharp focus on the issue of God's will for our lives.

When Christians plan, we are basically seeking to find and fulfill the will of God for our lives; a planning session is nothing more or less than a "seeking the mind of the Father session." The plans I adopt for the upcoming year should be the same plans that God ordained for my life eons ago. To speak of the will of God for my life and my personal goals for the new year is to discuss the same thing. This synonymity is critical to our understanding of the planning process. We don't plan according to our own understanding, and then ask God to bless those plans. We seek his will until we find it, and then we plan to obey it.

Finding God's Will

I'm convinced that God has a very intricate and detailed plan for each of our lives. He doesn't just give input on the "big events" and leave the minor issues to our discretion. On any given issue, he has an opinion, and for every question we face in life, he has an answer. But unfortunately, we seldom seek his will on a consistent basis. We treat God as though he runs a wrecker service—we call on him only when we're in a mess. The only time anyone ever asks my counsel relative to knowing God's will for their life is when they're facing a dramatically important decision. Several months ago a young man came to see me because he was having difficulty assessing God's will for his life relative to marriage. He seemed so con-

cerned about finding God's will in this issue. Regrettably,
prior to this time he didn't regularly seek the Lord. It
took a time of crisis to get his attention. Similarly, a
concerned mother sought my counsel about a wayward
daughter. I was tempted to say, "Why didn't you seek the
Lord's will for your daughter's life when she was an infant
and then channel her toward that purpose? Why have you
waited until a time of crisis to become concerned?" It is
unfortunate but true: the only time most Christians ever
seek the will of God for their lives is when they are forced
to make a decision in which the most favorable choice is
not extremely obvious. We leave this factor of "God's will"
out of focus until we are confronted with a crisis, indecision, or a choice of magnitudinous proportions and impact.

Strategic living is based upon discovering and fulfilling the will of God for our lives. Therefore, strategic living requires that the issue of God's will be kept in constant,
sharp focus. It's not something we seek periodically, but
it becomes a constant factor receiving our incessant attention. His will is no longer like the spare tire to be used
only in case of emergency; it's the hub of the wheel, an
expressed essential to our existence. Strategic living does
not lead us to frantically search for God's will on sporadic,
crisis-prompted occasions, but rather it allows us to com-
fortably walk day by day, knowing that his will has been
established as a prominent and constant factor in our
lives.

**Sixth, life planning/goal setting helps us dis-
cover our purpose in life and helps us accomplish the "big things."**

Sometimes it's hard to see the forest for the trees. We
get so involved in day-to-day activities that we fail to

observe what we're doing year to year or decade to decade.
It's like the pilot of a small airplane becoming so involved
in the mechanics of flying that he fails to keep track of
where he's going. He may be successful in maintaining
safe flying conditions but if he misses his final destination, the flight is unsuccessful. Many people are so concerned with making it day to day that they never stop to
get the big picture. They never discover their unique purpose in life.

In a general sense we all share the same *spiritual* purpose in life. This could be expressed in many biblical ways:

"To become conformed to the image of His Son" (Rom.
8:29)

"For to me, to live is Christ, and to die is gain" (Phil.
1:21)

". . . And whom I have created for My glory" (Isa. 43:7)

The Customized Purpose

In a more specific sense, God has a distinct direction,
a customized purpose, through which we can experience
the general purpose to which we are all called. W. A. Cris-
well is a pastor. God called him to be a pastor at a very
early age; he knew this was his purpose in life. Through
the years he had opportunities to be involved in politics,
business, evangelism, and other areas, but he always had
a resolute knowledge that his primary purpose in life was
to be a *pastor*. Tom Landry is a coach, Lee Iacocca is a
businessman, Leon Jaworski is a lawyer, Isaac Stern is a
violinist. What are you?

I don't want to imply that your calling needs to be of
a high professional level (doctor, lawyer) or that you must
be famous for what you do. Perhaps God has called you
to be a roofer, a housewife, a printer, or a schoolteacher.

I have a custodian friend who is totally content with his job, he performs his duties with exuberance and a sense of destiny. God has called him to serve as a custodian.

But there are many people who have never solidified this one major issue of life. If you ask them, "What has God called you to be or do?" they respond with a nebulous answer. Some people bounce around from job to job, viewing their employment only as a means of survival, not as a means of fulfilling their destiny. Some remain at a job long after the fulfillment has left, simply out of fear of change. Tragically, there are usually only two times in our lives when we ever consider the major direction which we will pursue. The first time is prior to college, when we're considering what major we want to pursue, and the other is after we graduate and we're searching for a job. For some young people, a job offered immediately after graduation from high school seems so inviting that they'll accept it, and by so doing they'll quell the very question of "what direction does God have for my life?" Even as adults, instead of waiting on God, determined not to move until he speaks, we usually respond to the first favorable set of circumstances.

And even when we do hear God's voice, what he calls us to do often seems so overwhelming that we don't know where to start. Life's purposes are usually that big, they seem out of our reach—things to be dreamed of but never achieved. Strategic living provides for the intelligent, calculated conquering of these formidable plans. It breaks down seemingly impossible goals into smaller, more achievable units. Discovering the purpose for which you were created is one issue, fulfilling that purpose is the flip side. Strategic living is a pathway to both.

Seventh, life planning/goal setting is scriptural. It is inherently spiritual.

Some Christians are strongly biased against planning. They think planning is a heathen practice from which spiritual-minded people are exempt. Their main argument is that planning is presumptuous. How can we plan for the future when only God knows the future? Actually, we presume upon God when we don't take the time to conscientiously seek his mind in regard to our future. Rest assured, that when we plan we're not stepping out of the "spiritual realm" into the area of the mundane but rather we're engaging in a spiritual practice that has plenty of biblical precedence.

Biblical Examples of Planning

God is a Master Planner. Have you ever noticed the planning which occurred during creation? Why did God create all that he did in six equal, consecutive series of events? Certainly, he could have created everything in a moment of time. And notice the logical order of creation. Could the fish have been created before the seas? Could man have preceded the earth which he inhabited? Of course not. God moved in a planned fashion when he created.

Let's consider some other biblical examples. The apostle Paul was an avid planner and strategist. He once said, "Forgetting what *lies* behind and reaching forward to what *lies* ahead, I press on toward the goal . . ." (Phil. 3:13–14). To the Corinthians, Paul said, "Run in such a way that you may win. Therefore I run in such a way, as not without aim" (1 Cor. 9:24, 26). Paul was so determined to fulfill his plans that he told the saints at Ephesus, "But I do not consider my life of any account as dear to myself, in order that I may finish my course" (Acts 20:24). He was so confident in his plans to visit Rome that even when his ship was wrecked enroute, it did not concern him; he was going to Rome. In essence, he said to the sailors on the ship, "Men, don't worry about whether we're going to make it or not, I *am* going to Rome, and this doesn't look like Rome."

Jesus lived a goal-oriented life. When he was on his way to Jerusalem, Jesus said, ". . . and the third *day* I reach My goal" (Luke 13:32). On the cross he was able to say, "It is finished!" (John 19:30). What was finished? With this shout of victory, Jesus proclaimed that the purpose for which he had come to earth—his primary goal in life—had been accomplished. Furthermore, his planned and deliberate work with the disciples resulted in the firm establishment of his kingdom. In other words, Jesus did not arbitrarily come to earth, wander around for thirty-three years doing kind deeds, and then impulsively decide to leave. His journey to earth was the execution of a complex divine plan; it fulfilled strategies designed in the heavenlies.

Nehemiah was a planner. While residing in a foreign land, he became burdened about the crumbled walls of Jerusalem and decided to do something about it. Following a night-time reconnaissance mission in which he surveyed the ruins and assessed the needs of the project, Nehemiah made some plans and challenged the people to do the work. Different sections of the work were organized and assigned to various families. As with every great work of God, there were those who opposed the endeavor, but demonstrating highly refined skills in leadership and organization, Nehemiah surmounted all opposition and completed the wall in the remarkable span of fifty-two days.

Nearly every book of the Bible is a commentary on the subject of planning. Consider the planning and building of Solomon's temple or the strategy that was developed to save the Jewish people during the time of Mordecai and Esther, or the military exploits of David and the other kings of Judah and Israel.

In summary, we must understand that planning *is* scriptural; it is not only permissible for Christians to be involved in planning, but also mandatory if we're to achieve our utmost potential for Christ and his kingdom.

Eighth, life planning/goal setting helps us make decisions and helps us make the right decisions.

I've discovered that conscientiously conceived decisions are more likely to be correct than impetuous decisions. Likewise, goals that are well thought-out are normally more plausible and advantageous than goals which are set quickly and then immediately pursued. Consider these biblical examples.

Samson was a very impetuous man and paid dearly for it. Concerning his first marriage, the Bible says he went down to Timnah and saw one of the daughters of the Philistines who "looked good" to Samson. He told his parents, "I saw a woman in Timnah . . . now therefore, get her for me as a wife" (Judg. 14:2). Against the counsel of his parents, Samson "got himself a wife" but it was to his own demise—the marriage lasted only a week.

David made an impulsive decision to commit immorality with Bathsheba, and the cost was great. It was not a well-thought-out, premeditated act; it was a rash spontaneous decision, and it was a wrong decision.

Lot "lifted up his eyes and saw all the valley of the Jordan, that it was well watered everywhere" (Gen. 13:10). Because of selfish desires, he quickly chose that land as his portion. That impulsive decision placed him near the city of Sodom. The evil influence of that city eventually led to the downfall of his family.

Life planning and goal setting helps us make right

decisions because well-thought-out plans are more likely
to be right than those made on the spur of the moment.
If you begin to seek God now about what to do the first
weekend of next month, you'll probably have a more viable weekend than if you wait until Saturday morning
and ask, "What should I do today?" If you decide in advance what to do with your income (develop a budget),
you'll stand a better chance of avoiding impulsive purchases and you'll have enough finances to meet all your
obligations.

Getting Control of Our Lives

Proper planning helps us to get control of our lives; we
plan our lives instead of having others plan for us. We're
able to avoid what writer Ted Engstrom (Engstrom 1984,
25) calls "the herd mentality." "Much of what motivates
us is little more than herd mentality. It's on the best-
seller list, so we read it. It's on the cover of our favorite magazine, so we wear it. It's featured in the gardening
magazine, so we grow it. A superstar touts it on television, so we buy it, or rent it, or eat it, or fly it!" The
major television networks have already decided what
many of you will be doing months from now, simply because they have already solidified their programming for
a particular Friday night, but you have put no thought
into the evening's activities. Consequently, on that Friday
night, you'll probably follow their plans by default; you
have no plans so you adopt theirs. *We need to gain control
of our lives.* Some people have a hard time saying *no* to
outside demands on their schedule. The best reason to say
no to someone is because a prior commitment has been
made. When asked "Would you speak at a fellowship this
Thursday evening?" I reply, "No, because I have a prior

commitment; I'm taking my wife to dinner." It's easier to make decisions when you're in control of your life.

During the planning process we establish policies, and policies also help us make right decisions. A policy is usually defined as a "standard answer for a recurring question." Policies are usually developed because someone gets tired of answering the same question many times. For instance, a child may ask day after day for a snack between meals. Finally the mother gets tired of answering the same question several times a day, so she establishes a policy: "Around this house there will be no snacks between meals." The child soon learns that it doesn't matter if it's Monday or Saturday, whether the refrigerator is full or empty, or whether Dad is home or not—there will be no snacks between meals. A mechanic might need to set a policy relative to loaning his tools to others. Sometimes the borrowers bring back the tools; sometimes they don't. Often, they're returned clean and in good shape; sometimes they're misused. He hesitates to say *yes* to some people and *no* to others, so he finally makes a policy statement: "I don't loan my tools." Regardless of who asks or what the need is, the decision has been made.

Policies need to be made in all areas of life. By making these major decisions, we eliminate having to make many minor decisions. For instance, in my family we have adopted several financial policies. We decided years ago that we would always give a tithe of our gross income to the church. Therefore every time I get paid, I don't have a decision to make; the decision has already been made. One month the bills may be unusually high—do we tithe? Yes, the decision has already been made. We may receive some unexpected income, should we tithe from this? It's not even necessary to ask the question because the answer is already settled. We have another financial policy that deals with debt. We have agreed never to purchase anything on credit that can't be paid off with budgeted funds in six months: every six months we're debt-free. If we're tempted to purchase an item but realize that it can't be purchased outright in six months, we don't buy it.

As a young boy, Daniel established a policy regarding the eating of unclean meat. I suspect that at an early age his Jewish mother taught him well regarding what the Mosaic law required concerning clean and unclean meat, and the eating of meat which had been offered to pagan gods. Daniel purposed in his heart that he would live or die by these convictions. He established a policy in this area of his life. Therefore, when confronted with a decision, even while captive in the court of King Nebuchadnezzar, he had an immediate reply: "But Daniel made up his mind that he would not defile himself with the king's choice food or with the wine which he drank" (Dan. 1:8). There is no indication that Daniel hesitated in his answer or that he had to go "pray about it"; he had established convictions in that particular area of his life.

In the planning process, conscientious policy statements are developed. They are continuous plans, plans that do not change, and they add stability to our lives. We should systematically establish policy statements for all major areas of our life. Here are some examples from just two areas.

Financial
1. Our family will operate on a yearly budget.
2. We will tithe from our gross income.
3. We will save 10 percent of our net income.
4. We will pay cash for everything.
5. We will purchase only top-quality merchandise.

Spiritual
1. I will honor the Bible as God's perfect Word.

2. I will be involved in a local church which is active and growing.
3. I will not drink alcoholic beverages, smoke, or otherwise submit my body to any harmful habit.
4. I will maintain a posture of continual spiritual growth by spending daily time with God.

With policies such as these, we eliminate the need to make many minor decisions. Suppose we are on vacation, staying in the home of a distant relative, and alcoholic beverages are served at dinner. Because the circumstances are different, do we consider partaking? No; much like the story of Daniel, a decision has already been made. Before the question surfaced, the answer was known.

Second Timothy 2:26 implies that Satan has a will for our lives. ". . . and they may come to their senses *and escape* from the snare of the devil, having been held captive by him to do his will." It's rather frightening to think that at times we may be fulfilling Satan's plan for our lives. The best protection against this dreaded possibility is to plan aggressively, based on the understanding we have of God's will for our lives. Whenever we drift into the arena of Satan's will, it's usually because we don't have the slightest notion of what God's will is. From this standpoint, proper planning can function as a protection device. It not only helps us make decisions and helps us make the right decisions, but it helps us to avoid bad decisions.

Ninth, life planning/goal setting works.

What About Your Future?

I often ask people, "*Where* are you going to be five years from now? *Who* are you going to be five years from now?"

Without effective life planning, the answer is quite predictable; you will be where and who you are today; there will be no significant change; it will be the same song, fifth verse (or worse yet, the fifth repetition of verse one). Ask yourself these questions: Where *will* you be five years from now—still in debt, perhaps, or in an unfulfilling job, overweight; still wishing you had finished college; procrastinating on starting a small business; not spending enough time with the kids; neglecting the reading of God's Word? And who *are* you going to be five years from now? Still tolerating a bad temper; facing the same marriage problems; underskilled; too timid to share your faith with others?

Without the aid of conscientious planning, our future will merely be an extension of the past. What you have been in the past is what you'll be in the future, or as someone has so aptly stated, "Choose your rut well, because you'll be in it for the next forty years."

David Swartz, management consultant, (Swartz 1983, 6, 7) uses a unique approach to illustrate this point.

> An obituary is supposed to be a brief history of a person's life. Usually, it gives only the barest details, such as date and place of birth, main accomplishments, occupation, and next of kin.
>
> For obvious reasons, most people do not like to write their obituaries. Nevertheless, I've turned obituary writing into a success-building concept for use in seminars for managers.
>
> Here's how it works. I ask the managers to write a summary of where they have been to date in their lives—with added information about family, friends, work and finances. Then I ask them to write projected versions of the rest of their lives based on past performances. I've learned that our past behavior is a good indicator of where we are headed unless we take positive corrective actions.

Get a clear picture of where you've been, what you've done, and who you are, and extrapolate that image over the next ten to twenty years of your life, and chances are that will be an accurate description of your future—unless, you make plans to alter your course.

One of the best reasons to recommend life planning/goal setting is that it works! It *really* works! I assure you!—if you will take the time (and it doesn't require a large amount of time) to list several things you want to see happen in the next six months and then conscientiously pursue those plans, in six months you'll be surprised at what you will have accomplished. To the contrary, if you don't take the effort to plan, in six months you will have accomplished exactly what you aimed at—nothing! It has been well stated: "He who aims at nothing usually hits it."

I'm convinced that once we've set a goal and have made a definite commitment to see that it is accomplished, we are halfway toward its fulfillment. Often just setting a goal will assure us of its completion. I'm not sure why this is so, but nevertheless it is true. Perhaps part of the reason lies in the fact that we have large reservoirs of untapped resources that lie dormant until they are activated toward a goal. Also, God has unlimited resources which are not tapped until we activate our faith toward a God-given goal.

I'm writing this chapter in September and I still have three months to complete the yearly goals and plans that I developed last December. I'm amazed that 90 percent of the plans have already been accomplished; I'm actually ahead of schedule. I'm amazed at how easy it was to accomplish many of the plans. If I had not set aside time last December to solidify and write down these plans, how many of them would have materialized? Probably very few.

Life planning/goal setting works! Get in on it—participate. You'll be glad you did. It may take several years to
fine tune your planning skills but that's all right; you'll
accomplish more in the process of learning than you would
ever have imagined. An old Chinese proverb says: "He
who aims for the stars shoots higher than he who aims
for the trees." Think big, aim high; even if you don't attain all of your ambitions, you will make progress in the
process of trying. And don't be afraid of failure. Usually,
every great accomplishment is preceded by failure and
defeat. On September 12, 1985, Pete Rose broke Ty Cobb's
venerated record: 4,191 career hits. But the media did not
mention the fact that Pete Rose also holds another record,
one for the most strikeouts: 9,518. I do believe that the
more skillful we become at goal setting, the higher our
success rate will be, but failure should never be viewed
as disabling or terminal. As in snow skiing, if you're not
falling down, you're not learning.

"*Que sera sera,* whatever will be will be" is a cute song
to sing but a lousy philosophy on which to build your life.
Decide now that you are going to be a planner. Adopt this
process as a part of your life. I've stated nine good reasons
why life planning/goal setting is advantageous; there are
many more, but nine should be enough. Begin now to be
involved; the investment in terms of time and effort is
minimal and the return is great.

Discussion Questions

These questions will help you analyze your personal planning habits. Carefully consider each one. It would be
helpful to discuss these questions with a friend or spouse.
Be honest with yourself!

1. Were your parents goal-oriented? Did they systematically develop plans in the major areas of their lives? How has their approach to planning affected you?
2. Are you satisfied with where you are in life? Do you feel like you're "behind, ahead, or about right"? (Consider areas like education, finances, professional status, spiritual, family, and so forth.)
3. If you wrote your own obituary based on past performance, what would it say? Are you satisfied? (See page 40).
4. Do you currently have a set of written plans? If not, why not?
5. List all the reasons you think life planning/goal setting is unnecessary.
6. List all the reasons you think life planning/goal setting would be advantageous.
7. Based on your response to questions five and six, are you willing to commit yourself to a systematic planning system?

2

Who Me?
Potential

ogo once philosophized, "We are surrounded by insurmountable opportunities." He was right; potential *is* all around
us. Wire, rocks, cardboard, land, air, tires,
intellect, needs, and old age all have one
thing in common—potential. But it usually takes a
trained, opportunistic eye to spot it.

Consider the man who used to bend and tear the
corners of his papers in order to hold them together
for filing. The frustration of this inadequate system and
the desire to find a better way led to the invention of the
paper clip.

Or how about the amateur rock hound in California
who was leaving his house to visit a rock show when his
two young sons each gave him five dollars with the instructions, "Daddy, buy me a pretty rock." When he ar-
rived at the show, he began rummaging through a large
box of "miscellaneous rocks" all priced at fifteen dollars
each. A large, uncut stone caught his attention and in
amazement he asked the vendor, "You want fifteen dollars

45

for *this* rock?" The vendor sheepishly answered, "All right,
ten dollars, and it's yours." Using his boys' money, he
bought a fifty-carat star sapphire which was valued at
$1.2 million dollars!

Possibility Thinkers

Recently two young Jewish boys, who had immigrated
from Israel, noticed that during the summer months
Americans burn their hands and bottoms when they sit
down in hot cars that have been out in the sun. Their
simple solution consisted of a folded piece of cardboard
placed on the dashboard, which would protect the car's
interior from the sun's scorching rays. Unable to sell their
idea to a major manufacturer, they began production in
their garage. In their second year they sold 2.4 million
car shades at $4.99 a piece. Whereas most of us only see
cardboard as useful for making boxes and sliding down
grassy hills, these two young men saw the possibilities
differently and are now experiencing the great American
dream.

During the Great Depression a man named Yates op-
erated a sheep ranch on the dusty plains of West Texas.
Times were hard, and had it not been for a government
subsidy, he would have defaulted on his mortgage pay-
ments. On the surface, the land was barely adequate to
feed a small flock of sheep. One day the exploration di-
vision of a major oil company approached Yates about
drilling a wildcat well on his land. Seismographic tests
indicated that there might be some black gold underneath
his nearly repossessed ranch. With nothing to lose, Yates
signed a lease contract.

The first well struck oil at 1,115 feet and flowed at
80,000 barrels a day. Subsequent wells produced twice
that amount. Thirty years later the oil was still flowing,

and tests showed that the wells were still capable of producing 125,000 barrels of oil a day.

For years, Yates had lived in poverty because of untapped resources. I'm not saying he was to blame—what does a sheep rancher know about oil—but there he was, living like a pauper, when all the time he had the potential of being a multimillionaire. There was great possibility in what he possessed, but it lay dormant for years until someone saw potential in some sheep-trodden, West Texas land.

And speaking of West Texas land, let's not forget the ingenious Vernon Holcomb, a rancher in Stanton, Texas, who went from raising herds of cattle to raising salt water shrimp and oysters. If that sounds strange, it is; Stanton, Texas, is five hundred miles from the Gulf of Mexico.

Vernon discovered that a few feet below his once fertile land ran a salty underground river, a result of salt deposited on the land millions of years ago. The seeping water soon polluted the once rich cotton fields and Vernon's cows had to look elsewhere for a drink. Instead of succumbing to the problem, he used a good dose of resourcefulness to turn a curse into a blessing.

He converted fifteen acres of his contaminated land into large salt water ponds where he raises and sells large shrimp and oysters. His business, Genesis Seafood Inc., now utilizes its own processing plant with two refrigerated box cars. His neighbors can purchase fresh shrimp right off the farm and other West Texans buy his product in frozen packages.

Vernon had an eye for opportunity and the courage to give it a try.

First Baptist Church-Dallas is located in the center of the Dallas skyline. Several years ago the church built a four-story parking garage adjacent to their church campus. The building received several awards for its architectural beauty.

Upon its completion, however, the church was hard pressed to service the debt incurred by the new building. One day a young engineer was contemplating the problem when his thoughts must have tilted to the right side of his brain (the creative side). He noticed that the church, through the years, had become surrounded by skyscrapers. That made sense, because when ground space is limited, air space becomes valuable. His creative solution: sell the air space above the newly completed garage. In the final arrangement, Lincoln Properties, a large development firm, bought the air rights above the parking garage for four million dollars. They also bought the garage itself but the church has unrestricted use of the building on Wednesdays and Sundays, and every day after 5:00 P.M. and receives a percentage of all revenues. The final package came to around twelve million dollars. Pretty good return for an airy idea! What most people saw as a playground for pigeons, one man saw as the solution to a big problem.

Or consider the entrepreneurial eye of J. A. Jamison, owner of a tire-salvage operation called Tire Mountain. His 8 million used tires are valued at 3.2 million dollars. Jamison sells some of the tires to recappers and others to parks for playground equipment. While most of us are irritated at the inconvenience caused by bad tires, J. A. makes a handsome profit from them. That's because he saw *potential*.

Have you ever wondered how the hot dog was invented? A German immigrant, living in Philadelphia during the 1930s, made his living selling knockwurst (a thick, spicy sausage) and sauerkraut to the patrons of his small restaurant. In order to eliminate the expense of plates and silverware, one day he slit a German roll down the middle and served the sausage and sauerkraut inside the roll. That was the origination of our American obsession with tube steak. A German merchant, trying to save a little money, saw the potential in combining two cylindrically shaped food items. The possibility had been there for years, but one day—he saw it!

The potential which can be found in inanimate objects is paltry, however, when compared to the potential which is resident inside every human being. Man's three-pound brain is the most complex, orderly, and capable arrangement of matter known in the universe. Scientist Paul Weiss estimates that we have as many cells in our brain as there have been seconds in time since our part of the cosmos began—about one quadrillion. (That's one [1], followed by 15 zeros.) Whereas scientists used to think that we use no more than 5 percent of our brain's capacity, they now estimate that we only use one-tenth of 1 percent. Regardless of what the percentage is, we have a lot upstairs that we're not using.

Advice of an Angel

I grew up in a poor part of town. There weren't a lot of overachievers living in my neighborhood, and high self-esteem and confidence were two character traits that were more elusive than obvious in local residents. This environment was not conducive to developing confidence and optimism in a young boy—but I will never forget an encounter I had one day that, in retrospect, changed my life.

I would spend many summer afternoons skipping rocks and drowning minnows in the nearby creek. One day I made my daily trip down the dirt road that ran parallel to the creek, and saw an old man changing the oil in his car. I don't remember what started our conversation but

I'll never forget one bit of advice he repeated over and over. He said, "Young boy, you can do anything you set your mind to do. You can do anything. Do you want to be a lawyer? You can do it. Do you want to be a doctor? You can be one! You can do anything you set your mind to do!"

Do you believe in angels? I do. And if I've ever had an encounter with one, I think it must have happened that day. The old man spoke with much confidence, although it appeared that he had a very modest lifestyle. Angel— or mere mortal—I don't know, but I do know that those phrases became etched in granite on the tablets of my mind. It was a high impact experience that profoundly influenced my thinking and probably altered the outlook and the course of my life. The old man's words "You can do anything you set your mind to do" established in my heart the confidence factor. To this day, I believe that *all of us can do whatever we want to do.*

The truth is, potential is not the limiting factor in life. We all have enough potential to do whatever we want. Very seldom can we ever use the excuse "I just don't have what it takes." The problem is, we don't use what we have. Or, as Linus (Charlie Brown's sidekick) once philosophized: "Life is like a ten-speed bicycle. Most of us have gears we never use!"

"But," the conservative critic would muse, "there *are* things for which you lack potential. At age thirty-six, try to win the Olympic gold medal in the one-hundred-meter-sprint!" The point is, I don't *want* to win the Olympic gold medal in the one hundred-meter-sprint. That's not one of my aspirations; it's not my heart's desire; it's not in my realm of interest. Normally, our hearts will not crave after things outside our reach. God will not create in us a desire that cannot be fulfilled. We will seldom set goals which are beyond our reach. The point I am making is *not:* "You can do anything," but rather, "You can do anything you *want* to do." There's a *big* difference.

Overcomers

Let me illustrate my point by giving several examples of how different individuals fulfilled their dreams and aspirations, many of them despite seemingly insurmountable obstacles.

Charles Schulz failed every subject in the eighth grade! Due to constant rejection, he was a social hermit. The one thing he was good at was drawing; he had a talent in art. Trying to make good with his ability, he applied for a cartoonist job at Walt Disney Studios. He was told that he wasn't good enough. Undaunted, he began to sketch out the frustrations of his life through the cartoon character of Charlie Brown. Charles Schulz's deep desire to artistically express himself and his fortitude to overcome obstacles have given us the comic strip "Peanuts."

Jack LaLanne was for years the guru of physical fitness. Even at sixty-five, he could do 1,033 pushups in twenty-three minutes and swim a mile while towing 13 rowboats filled with 76 people. His childhood, however, was quite different. As a young boy he suffered from several physical maladies. He had flat feet, a bad back, boils, and headaches so bad that he would often bang his head against the wall. One day, after being challenged by the energetic speech of a nutritionist/physical-fitness expert, he determined that his life would change. He began exercising and following a strict diet. His life did change, as did the lives of many of his followers.

Or how about Wilma Rudolph? Born prematurely, she nearly died from pneumonia and scarlet fever, and she was crippled by polio. The doctors gave her little hope

that she would ever be able to *walk*—much less run. But
deep in her heart she was determined not only to walk,
but to run, and to make her mark in the world of sports.
Against all odds, she began to pursue her dream. When
her parents weren't watching, she would take off her
braces and try to walk unassisted. To the amazement of
her doctors and friends, she began to compete in track
and field events. Her crowning achievement occurred before 80,000 fans in Rome, Italy, at the 1960 Summer
Olympic Games. When she entered the stadium, the fans
chanted, "Wilma! Wilma! Wilma!" In one of the great
moments in Olympic history, Wilma Rudolph became the
first woman to win three Olympic gold medals. Despite
many obstacles, she tapped into the limitless reservoir of
human potential and fulfilled her dream.

You're never too old or too poor to maximize your potential in life. Case in point: "Colonel" Harlan Sanders.
At the age of 66, when most people are thinking about
retirement or death or some stage in between, he decided
to take action. He was almost broke, and his only source
of income was a $105 a month check from Social Security.
He did remember, however, the tasty fried chicken his
mother used to serve when he was a boy. With a flash of
entrepreneurial energy he began selling franchises for
that special chicken recipe. His first restaurant in Salt
Lake City was an instant success. The rest of the story
is obvious; we've been licking our fingers ever since. Age
was no barrier for Mr. Sanders; when times were tough
he took the initiative to set some goals and work for their
fulfillment.

When talking about human potential, my favorite il-
lustration is that of John Goddard's life. A feature article
in the March 24, 1972, issue of *Life* magazine told his
story.

At age fifteen, John Goddard wrote down 127 goals which he wanted to accomplish in his lifetime. Included in these goals were: climb Mounts Kilimanjaro, Ararat, Fuji, McKinley (and thirteen others); visit every country in the world; learn to fly an airplane; retrace the travels of Marco Polo and Alexander the Great; visit the North and South Poles, Great Wall of China, Taj Mahal (and other exotic areas); become an Eagle Scout; dive in a submarine; play flute and violin; publish an article in *National Geographic* magazine; learn French, Spanish, and Arabic; milk a poisonous snake; read the entire *Encyclopaedia Britannica;* and other goals, similar in variety and scope.

At age 47, Goddard had accomplished 103 of these goals and was in the process of completing several others. Goddard was neither wealthy nor gifted when he began his amazing saga of adventure and accomplishment. He was just a fifteen-year-old boy who believed all things were possible and that he had the potential to do what he wanted to do.

Clement Stone was right when he said, "What the mind can conceive and believe in, the mind can achieve."

But not only is there potential in the physical realm and in the psyche of man, the spirit of man is brimming with possibilities. Have you ever considered the implications of the preposition "in" as found in these verses?

". . . Christ *in* you, the hope of glory" (Col. 1:27).

"Now to Him who is able to do exceeding abundantly beyond all that we ask or think, according to the power that works with*in* us" (Eph. 3:20).

". . . the kingdom of God is *in* your midst" (Luke 17:21). (Italics added in these verses.)

The spiritual dynamics of the universe are not deposited in a heavenly vault. They reside in those who believe that Jesus is the Lord. Talk about gaining a competitive edge; if you are a Christian you have the power that raised Jesus from the dead—within you. If we thought about that for very long, it would overload our circuits. To say that the presence of Jesus in our lives makes a difference in our potential level is the understatement of the year. When we become a Christian, we plug into unlimited resources. And what a difference that makes.

When you consider the dormant potential that is *around* you and then the much larger pool of resources that is *in* you, there remains no excuse for inactivity, apathy, or underachievement. Life can and should be filled with continuous, meaningful activity.

Again, I'm *not* saying you can conquer the world. I *am* saying you can conquer *your* world. You can achieve. You can be a success. You can live a highly productive, satisfying life.

This was Paul's approach to life when he said, "I can do all things through Him who strengthens me" (Phil. 4:13). He begins by saying, "I can do all things," but then adds a restrictive, clarifying clause, "through Him who strengthens me." Whatever God asks us to do, he will give us the strength to do it. If you don't have the voice to sing opera with the Met, God never intended you to sing opera. But more times than not, our problem is not that we attempt things that are out of our reach, we normally don't reach far enough. We shortchange ourselves because we are not confident of our potential. Balderdash!

You have the potential to do great things. Potential is around you and in you. Start excavating and you will discover your lode. And the answer to the question, "Who, *me*?" is "Yes, *you!*"

Discussion Questions

These questions will help identify your personal assessment of your potential. Spend adequate time answering
each one. Again, it would help to discuss the questions
with a friend or spouse.

1. What is *potential*?
2. How is potential identified and used?
3. Do you see potential in yourself and the resources
   around you?
4. Is there a relationship between what you perceive as
   lack of potential and areas of underachievement in
   your life?
5. What does this verse say to you—in terms of potential? "Now to Him who is able to do exceeding abundantly beyond all that we ask or think, according to
   the power that works within us" (Eph. 3:20).
6. How do pessimism and negativism affect potential?
7. List all your personal resources (such as talents, skills,
   spiritual gifts, heritage, finances, abilities, influence,
   friends, and so forth). Do you see untapped potential
   in these resources?
8. Are you willing to plan with a mind-set on unlimited
   potential rather than on limited resources?

3

Who Pushed Me?
Motivation

*T*he story is told of the old town drunk who left the tavern late at night and decided to take the shortcut home, even though it meant walking through the graveyard. There were no moon or stars to light the ground, and with his cautiousness hampered by inebriation, he tripped and fell into an open grave prepared for the next day's funeral. He was immediately stone sober. He began a frantic attempt to scale the side walls, but the dirt only crumbled in his hands. After several unsuccessful attempts, he decided to wait until dawn—someone would arrive and help him out. So he sat in the corner and began to doze off. But soon, another town drunk, also hoping to shorten his walk home, stumbled into the same grave. The newcomer had the same first reaction as his predecessor; he started jumping toward the top, clawing at the dirt, trying to escape.

Realizing the man's attempts would be futile, and wanting to spare him the trouble, the first drunk said, "Friend, you'll never get out of here."

But he did.

It's amazing what you can do—if you're motivated. And it's equally amazing what you can't do if you're not motivated. The presence or absence of motivation is often the sole difference between energized action and accomplishment, and apathetic inactivity and failure.

As discussed in the previous chapter, incompetence is seldom the limiting factor. But if everyone has great potential, why are most people underachievers? A primary reason is motivation, or more accurately stated—the lack of motivation.

Defining Motivation

But before we talk about motivation, let's shoot down three terms which have often been misconstrued as being synonymous with motivation. True motivation does not claim them as partners.

Intimidation

This is where the boss tries to portray a "bigger than life" caricature. Using a title or position (which he probably doesn't deserve) or using knowledge (usually a very narrow field of knowledge), he uses leverage to produce results. Fear and condemnation are the tools of his trade, and threats are the common expressions. "Do this, or this will happen," he says.

Using this approach, results are often attained but the work environment is rotten. Also, the high level of employee turnover makes you question whether it really works or not.

Manipulation

In this scenario, the boss achieves the end result (production), but he doesn't care at all about the means to the end. Half-truths and subtle innuendos are the tools of his

trade, as he uses people like the pieces of a chess game.
I've discovered that people can't stand to be manipulated
and will avoid it like the bubonic plague. They feel used
and resent it.

Stimulation

In this approach the emotions are targeted. It may be
a sad story, a thrilling anecdote, or just a highly stimu-
lating presentation. The only problem is, when the emotions go back to a normal level, the impetus created during
such stirring moments also leaves. A pastor may present
a moving message on soul winning and during the invi-
tation get a multitude of people to commit to Monday-
night visitation, but a month later—where are the people? The stimulation has worn off.

There is only one good path to consistent, quality
achievement—*motivation*.

Motivation is internal; it *starts* from within. It is logical; it makes sense (although in time it can become
emotional). And motivation is lasting; it won't wear off.

For sure, the term has been misused. We often hear,
"He's a great motivational speaker!" Actually, he's probably a great stimulator. I'm not sure there is such a thing
as a motivational speaker, because it's not something that
we receive externally; it's something that clicks internally.

Paul J. Meyer, President of Success Motivation Insti-
tute, says, "If you want to achieve permanent, sustaining
success, the motivation that will drive you toward that
goal must come from within. It must be personal, deep-
rooted and a part of your innermost thoughts. All other
motivation, the excitement of a crowd, the stimulation of
a pep talk, the exhilaration of a passing circumstance is
external and temporary. It will not last."

Don't go through life continually having to be intimi-

dated, manipulated, or stimulated. Get motivated. You'll
have more energy and vision than you thought possible.
People won't have to push you—they'll have to get out of
your way!

A wise employer will take time to consider what will
motivate his employees. He'll then discover the key to
productivity. Eisenhower said, "Leadership is the ability
to get people to do what you want because they want to
do it."

But this isn't a book on management; it's a book on
personal planning and goal setting. So the question is:
"What motivates you?" One of the reasons we're underachievers is that we're not *motivated*. Motivation is the
combination that unlocks a vault of untapped resources.
It's the on/off switch that operates a huge, almost limitless machine—you!

Motivation Is Personal

But what motivates us? Only you can answer that. If
you're hungry, you're probably motivated to find food. If
you're a millionaire, you may be motivated to make another million, or you may be motivated to take art lessons.
If you were like Mother Teresa, you would be motivated
to care for the lepers of India. Several years ago, I was
motivated to run the New York Marathon. I had never
jogged consistently in my life. What in the world caused
me to subject myself to the pain and distress of running
26.2 miles? I don't really know, other than I was motivated to do it. My sister has been attending night school
for ten years working toward a degree in interior design.
Why has she persevered through such a difficult path
while others dropped out? When I asked her, she answered, "I've always wanted a degree in interior design."

She has been gripped by that mysterious, often unexplainable element—motivation.

I'm just not sure that there is a strict formula for acquiring motivation. It's highly personal and therefore it's often difficult to identify all the elements that combine to produce the motivation factor. Past experiences, future hopes, present pressures, a magazine article, a deep conviction, the example of a hero, the suggestion of a friend, a personal preference, a selfish desire, a vision from God, a natural talent—all these and more can combine to produce—motivation.

But one thing is certain: motivation is an essential ingredient for productivity, so we better catch this elusive bug. Here are several suggestions that will help create optimum conditions for its development.

People Support What They Help to Create

This is a law of management which managers should use whenever possible and to whatever degree is feasible. I realize that occasionally (usually due to time restraints) the boss must say, "Do this *this* way," but the results are always better when people are allowed to participate in the planning process. When they have had input into a plan, they will help defend it and see it to fruition. Those who will be involved in the execution of plans should always be included in their development.

The same applies to individual achievement. Motivation is more likely to be spawned when we develop our own plans than if they are forced upon us. Whenever I'm counseling someone about life planning, I'm always careful not to do the planning for them. I may make some suggestions to light the pilot light, but the real flame of desire must be generated from within.

Even in raising children it's best to wait for personal

initiative. Music lessons are often initiated with these words: "You *will* take piano lessons; you *will* practice regularly, and you *will* enjoy it." Such strict navigation usually results in shipwreck. Why not ask your child what instrument she would like to play? Or more fundamental than that, ask her if she even wants to play an instrument. In order to expose her to the music world, you may want to take her to a concert, or let her hear an instrument played by a professional, but wait until something clicks inside of her before you make lessons mandatory.

In raising children I realize there must be a balance between voluntary and required action. We can't wait until they're "motivated" to go to school before we send them, and we can't make school attendance dependent on daily feelings—there are areas that require direct control. But even in these areas we would be wise to teach our children the value and necessity of certain factors and to try to eliminate hindrances to motivation. (These will be discussed later in this chapter.)

So let me suggest that you look deep within for that spark of motivation. Don't wait to be told to do something; discover something *you* want to do. If you come up with an idea, you will defend it, stick with it, and work overtime to achieve it.

Motivation Is Contagious

If you want to be motivated, get around motivated people. I'm not talking about "motivational speakers" or "excitable people" or anyone who has more rah-rah than they do productivity. I'm referring to people who really produce.

Someday I want to spend time with Jamie Buckingham, my favorite Christian author. He's written forty books in the past sixteen years, and all of them with award-winning craftsmanship. Just being around the man would quicken my writing pace. Or how about John Goddard, who was mentioned in the previous chapter? Stepping into his world would make all of us seem like we're in slow motion.

Yes, motivation can be contagious. If we make an effort to place ourselves in the midst of motivated, achieving people, their example will act as a catalyst for our latent potential. It's like throwing a cold charcoal briquet into a roaring fire; it soon heats up to its environment.

It's also good to visit with high achievers because they challenge our status quo. Norms are always relative. You may think you're doing pretty well compared to those around you, but put yourself in a different crowd and you may realize you've been coasting. A friend of mine who is a builder has the fastest work pace I've ever seen. He has three phones on his desk and often uses all three at one time, and that's hard to do with two ears. He can juggle more balls at once than anyone I know. When I step into his world, it makes my pace look like slow motion. He motivates me.

Planning Generates Motivation

How long has it been since you've participated in a brain-storming session? The next time you're faced with a difficult problem, ask three or four of your free-thinking friends to join you for a cup of coffee. Share your problem and then sit back and take notes. Ideas begin to burst forth like popcorn over an open fire. And soon in the midst of ideas, suggestions, and plans, motivation will emerge. Planning generates motivation.

I'm seldom motivated to plan but I'm always motivated as the result of the planning process. Planning must be done as an act of the will; it is something we should schedule to do on a regular basis. We must plan to plan.

Most people never participate in formal planning. They may plan on the spur of the moment, or when they're mowing the grass, (and granted, many fine plans have come from such moments), but formal planning doesn't exist. When was the last time you devoted an hour of your day, solely to planning? When we plan we assess our resources, we become future-oriented, we become unified and committed, and we consider our potential. All these help produce motivation. I recently participated in a weekend retreat with church leaders. Prior to the retreat, motivation was at a low ebb. After the retreat, motivation was at high tide. The difference? *Planning*.

If you lack motivation, chances are you haven't been planning. Set aside an hour in your schedule next week for the sole purpose of planning. As we tinker with the mechanics of planning, that mysterious, elusive force called *motivation* will begin to surface.

We Are Motivated by Meaningful Action

Years ago a psychologist conducted an experiment that illustrates the fact that we are motivated by meaningful action.

He hired four men and paid them a good wage to work eight hours a day. Their task: dig a trench two feet wide, two feet deep, and twenty feet long. When they finished, they were told to fill the trench with dirt, move over four feet and dig another trench, the same dimensions as the first.

After two days of repeating this meaningless task, two of the men quit, and the psychologist doubled the hourly wage of the two men who remained. But after two more days, they also quit. It wasn't the hard work that made them quit; nor was it inadequate financial remuneration—they just couldn't tolerate investing their time and energy into a project that obviously lacked direction and ultimate purpose.

We're motivated the most when we're involved in meaningful activities, particularly activities that relate to a greater goal. Motivation would not come easy if you had to take a college physics course as an isolated class. If, however, it was a prescribed course toward a medical degree, it would be viewed as a means toward an end. If the end was greatly desired, it would provide enough motivation necessary to complete the course.

A housewife may be motivated to exercise several times a week because she values a trim, fit physique. A young man may be motivated to get up early in the morning and deliver papers because he's saving for a new motorcycle. A businessman will take night courses to finish a graduate degree, so he can apply for a management position. In all these examples motivation is present, not because the specific activities are enjoyable (who likes to sweat, get up at 5:00 AM, or miss Monday Night Football?), but because the activities meaningfully relate to something in the future.

Whenever possible, present activities need to relate to future goals. This not only enhances our level of hope and expectation, but it gives order and permanence to our daily activities. Each activity becomes like a piece of a large jigsaw puzzle. The longer we live, the more complete the picture becomes. Past experiences are not fragments to be discarded but essential pieces of a master plan.

Needs Motivate

Abraham Maslow, in his book *Motivation and Personality,* (New York: Harper & Row, 1954), developed a framework of human needs. According to Maslow, there is a hierarchy of needs that we're all motivated to satisfy.

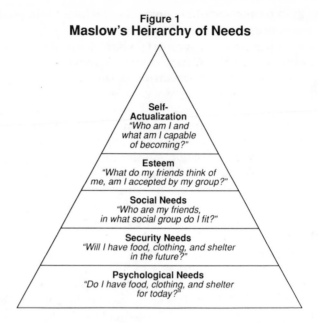

Figure 1
Maslow's Heirarchy of Needs

We typically start at the bottom of the pyramid and work our way up (see figure 1).

Physiological

These needs include the basic elements required to sustain life—food, clothing, and shelter. Until satisfied, they obviously have the highest degree of importance. The majority of a person's activities (and motivation) will be focused at this level until these needs are met. The basic question is "Do I have food, clothing, and shelter for today?"

Security

Once physiological needs are met, safety and security needs become predominant. We want to avoid physical

danger and the possible deprivation of our basic physiological needs. This includes the need for job security,
maintaining personal property such as a house or auto,
and concern for the future. The basic question is "Will I
have food, clothing, and shelter in the future?"

Social

When our physiological needs are met and if we feel
confident that we are safe and secure, we'll then concentrate on the next level of needs—social. Most people want
to interact with others in situations where they feel com-
fortable and accepted. Social needs include the need for
love and acceptance and human contact. The basic question is "Who are my friends/in what social group do I fit?"

Esteem

But once we are satisfied with our social affiliation, the
next issue is recognition, or esteem. We want to be more
than just a member of the group; we need to be recognized
and respected by others. Satisfaction of these needs may
produce feelings of self-confidence, self-respect, prestige,
power, and respect from others. The basic question is
"What do my friends think of me; am I accepted by my
group?"

Self-Actualization

When all the other needs are met (or at least partially
met), Maslow suggests that we're ready to maximize our
potential—to become self-actualized. He says it this way:
"What a man *can* be, he *must* be." A teacher must teach,
a musician must perform music, a writer must write, a
general must win battles. The need for self-actualization
includes the need to grow, to feel self-fulfilled, and to re-

alize one's potential. The basic question is: "Who am I/what am I capable of becoming?"

Maslow is a secular psychologist. It might be good then to see if his theory is in plumb with the Word of God. There's no doubt that his research accurately reflects society and basic human behavior, but sometimes society and basic human behavior are not consistent with God's ideal.

A biblical response to the first need in the hierarchy—that of physiological needs—might be Matthew 6:31–33, "Do not be anxious then, saying, 'What shall we eat?' or 'What shall we drink?' or 'With what shall we clothe ourselves?' For all these things the Gentiles eagerly seek; for your heavenly Father knows that you need all these things. But seek first His kingdom and His righteousness; and all these things shall be added to you." Jesus acknowledges that these basic needs exist, but he assures us that they will be met as we focus on spiritual priorities.

What does the Lord have to say about the second level of needs—safety and security? Philippians 4:6 and 19 say, "Be anxious for nothing, but in everything by prayer and supplication with thanksgiving let your requests be made known to God. And my God shall supply all your needs according to His riches in glory in Christ Jesus." In these verses I don't hear the Lord denying our concern for the future. He simply says that our hope and trust should be placed in him.

The need for social affiliation and self-esteem is addressed in First Corinthians 12 in which Paul discusses the importance of the body of Christ and its individual members.

"For even as the body is one and *yet* has many members, and all the members of the body, though they are many, are one body, so also is Christ. For the body is not one member, but many. If the foot should say, 'Because I am not a hand, I am not *a part* of the body,' it is not for this reason any the less *a part* of the body. And if the ear should say, 'Because I am not an eye, I am not *a part* of the body,' it is not for this reason any the less *a part* of the body. If the whole body were an eye, where would the hearing be? If the whole were hearing, where would the sense of smell be? But now God has placed the members, each one of them, in the body, just as He desired. And if they were all one member, where would the body be? But now there are many members, but one body. And the eye cannot say to the hand, 'I have no need of you'; or again the head to the feet, 'I have no need of you.' Now you are Christ's body, and individually members of it" (vv. 12, 14–21, 27).

The truth is—we *do* need each other. It's important to understand our role in the body of Christ and to fulfill that role. God doesn't want any hermits in his church. We need a sense of belonging and worth.

A modern-day paraphrase of self-actualization is "Be all that you can be." I don't think God has a problem with that, either. Paul said it this way to young Timothy, "Fulfill your ministry" (2 Tim. 4:5). God has a specific will for our lives, he has a separate, customized plan for each of us. Yes, he wants all of us to be holy, but he may want one person to be a holy lawyer and someone else a holy housewife. When we discover what God has created us to "be," we become self-actualized. The ultimate sense of fulfillment in life comes as we are confident that we are experiencing that unique niche that God has created for us.

How does all this relate to motivation? To the degree that needs motivate, we will be motivated to work through Maslow's hierarchy or a somewhat altered hierarchy, based upon scriptural influence. Where are you on the pyramid, what is your next step up?

Why do some people stop after their basic needs are satisfied? Motivation runs high when your stomach is growling, when the kids don't have shoes, or when you lose your job, but many people fail to climb the summit of Maslow's pyramid. And why are some people unmotivated even though they are surrounded by motivated, achieving people? And why do even well-conceived plans often fail to provide adequate motivation?

It could be that they were stymied by one of the hindrances to motivation.

Hindrances to Motivation

Fear of Failure

We all have our "comfort zone"—that safe area in which we've had past successes and in which we're not intimidated. We're often afraid to set out into the "unknown zone" because we don't want to fail. And the fear of failure always stifles the flow of motivation.

Who said failure is a bad thing? Failure is actually a necessary step toward achievement. A pole-vaulter may fail ten times before he finally makes it over the top. Musical practice is just a series of constant failures. We practice a scale or passage of music, failing all the while, until we can finally execute it well, and then we progress to a more difficult passage that we can fail at. If you ever stop failing, and just do the things you already do well, you'll stop progressing. Failure due to sloppiness, slothfulness, or lack of effort is unacceptable, but failure experienced while striving for achievement is commendable.

Theodore Roosevelt wrote this about failure:

> It is not the critic who counts; not the man who points
> out how the strong man stumbled or where the doer of
> deeds could have done them better. The credit belongs to
> the man who is actually in the arena; whose face is marred
> by dust and sweat and blood; who strives valiantly; who
> errs, and comes up short again and again, because there
> is no effort without error and shortcoming; who does ac-
> tually try to do the deed; who knows the great enthusiasm,
> the great devotion and spends himself in a worthy cause;
> who, at the worst, if he fails at least fails while daring
> greatly. Far better it is to dare mighty things, to win glo-
> rious triumphs even though checkered by failure, than to
> rank with those poor spirits who neither enjoy nor suffer
> much because they live in the gray twilight that knows
> neither victory or defeat. (Engstrom 1984, 75)

In order to overcome the fear of failure, use a little
reverse psychology. Plan to do something this week so
different and so far out of your comfort zone that you're
bound to fail. And when you fail, receive it—even enjoy
it! But use that failure to learn something—to make
yourself a better person. Thomas Huxley said, "It is gen-
erally understood that we usually learn more from our
mistakes than from our successes."

Complacency

Complacency is an unhealthy satisfaction with one's
current status. It usually occurs when we set goals and
standards which are not challenging, or when we've already achieved a degree of success and we're now satisfied
to rest on our laurels.

Success can only be measured in terms of our capacity.
To ask, "What have you accomplished in the past five
years?" will result in incomplete data. We must also ask,
"What *could* you have accomplished in the past five years?"

Then we can determine if complacency has set in. If you have three goals for tomorrow—get up, eat, and go to bed—you'll probably achieve all three but to say you've had a productive day would be stretching the point. If we continually set and achieve only nonchallenging goals, we may develop a false sense of productivity, which leads to complacency.

On the other hand, many people have already set and accomplished many admirable goals, but now complacency has crept in and all they talk about is their trophy case. They remain oriented to the past and seldom think of the future.

There are also those who are baffled and frustrated because their goals seem elusive and impossible. These people are not complacent because they have already achieved their goals, but because they think they never will. In any case, complacency will paralyze motivation.

Laziness

Laziness is sin. It should be placed in the same category as anger, greed, or any other attitude that offends God. If convicted, we need to admit it and quit it. Here's a quick laziness test:

1. Do you sleep too much?
2. Do you procrastinate?
3. Do you look for excuses to avoid work?
4. Do you only do what's necessary or required and never more?
5. Do you lack initiative?
6. Do you plan each day's activities or do you just "do what comes up"?
7. Do you end the day without having accomplished anything? (For instance, what *did* you do yesterday?)

Slothfulness causes a log jam in our flow of motivation. A lazy person will not be motivated to do anything—he is content to just "get by."

Complacency and laziness are habit forming, and they are both obstacles to motivation.

Procrastination

Many good plans, fueled by vision and inspiration, have been derailed by procrastination. And though it can strike at any time, procrastination usually tries to subvert our plans at the very beginning. Procrastination knows that a long journey must begin with a single step, so it will try to prevent that first step.

How many times have you heard the statement, "I'm going to do that someday—when I get around to it?" That's procrastination. I have a friend who has been "going to write a book" for ten years. Procrastination has his good plan paralyzed. If he would just sit down and begin writing, he would probably have a first draft manuscript within a year.

On a more personal note, I have wanted to give my daughter piano lessons for several years. But we don't have a piano in our house, and piano lessons without a piano to practice on can be counterproductive. I need to buy a piano. This is the first step toward Lauren being the next Rubinstein of her generation! But the plan has bogged down in the quicksand of procrastination.

There's one simple solution to procrastination:

DO IT *now!*

Identify the first small step that will begin your journey and then do it! Do what? Do *it!* Do it when?

DO IT *now.*

Substitute a specific activity for that tiny pronoun, and then do it! Don't put it off any longer. If possible, put this book down and

DO IT *NOW.*

If not now, put it on your schedule for tomorrow.

Beware of procrastination—it is the adversary of motivation.

Stagnation

It's easy to become stagnant. We develop a daily routine, we talk to the same people, we drive down the same streets, we go to the same restaurants, and soon our daily habits and mundane procedures begin to infuse our system with an imperceptible amount of anesthetic which, over a period of time, renders our motivation level listless and inept.

When our lives get stuffy and stale, we need to open the windows and let in some fresh air. Along with fresh stimulation will come motivation. Here are some suggestions:

Stimulate your mind. When was the last time you read a book, cover to cover? (Shame on most of you.) When was the last time you read a book that didn't deal with your profession? Read, read, read. In addition to my daily Bible readings, I read one newspaper daily, two magazines weekly, five other magazines monthly, and two books a month. Reading is the best mind stimulant available. Tomorrow go to the library or bookstore and get some books to read.

Another good source of mental stimulation is listening to audio cassettes. Research from the University of Southern California indicates that you can acquire the equivalent of two years of college education in three years

by listening to cassette tapes in the car, assuming that
you drive at least twelve thousand miles per year. You
can find tapes on any subject you want. Plug in and re-
fresh yourself.

Attending meetings and seminars will also provide a
fresh breeze across your mind. In every major metropol-
itan area (particularly if a college is nearby), there are
numerous opportunities to attend seminars and conferences. It takes effort to break out of our daily routine,
but the results are worth it.

Interact with new people. Has your normal "modus op-
erandi" restricted you to a small group of friends and
associates? If so, make an effort to meet new people. That
doesn't mean you have to forsake your old buddies—just
meet new ones. Call that colleague who works across town
and invite him to lunch. Have your neighbor over for a
glass of tea. Form a dinner club with four other couples
and meet together every other month. For some, meeting
new people is an intimidating proposition but it's always
worth the effort.

Alter your daily schedule, visit new locations. Instead
of coming directly home from work, go to the library, or
go skip rocks in the lake. Just do *something* different. If
you take a sack lunch to work, don't always eat in the
employees' cafe; eat outside under a tree or at a local
park. When you're driving to work, take a different route.
Plan weekend trips to areas of interest, or to areas that
don't seem interesting and make them interesting.

When you're chopping wood with an ax, you have to
stop periodically to sharpen the blade. Otherwise, the
harder you work the more ineffective you become. When
our lives become dull and stagnant, motivation wanes,
and soon we become ineffective. Stagnation is a hin-
drance to motivation.

So the words of exhortation are—*get motivated*. Eliminate the hindrances to motivation, embrace those activities which promote motivation—and get motivated. Look for, pray for, that fire that burns within. You won't accomplish many meaningful things in life without the motivation factor.

The story is told of an elderly man who was taking his first ocean voyage. One afternoon a storm blew in, and a young lady lost her balance and fell overboard. Immediately there was another person overboard and, to everyone's amazement, it was the old man. He helped the girl stay afloat until a lifeboat could be launched, and the two of them picked up.

That evening the captain hosted a reception in honor of the old man to celebrate his heroic rescue. The other passengers were enthusiastic and generous with their words of kindness and appreciation.

Soon someone said, "Speech! Speech!" The old man hadn't said a word up to this point and was rather embarrassed at all the show of attention. He gingerly made his way to the podium and said, "There's just one thing I want to know—who pushed me?"

Hopefully, our push will come from within.

Discussion Questions

1. What motivates you?
2. Recall several instances in your life in which you were highly motivated. What was the catalyst for motivation in these cases?
3. Identify someone you know who would be described as a motivated individual. Analyze that person's life; if possible, visit with him/her and find out what makes that person tick.

4. At which level are you in Maslow's hierarchy of needs? (Page 66).
5. Is there an area of your life in which progress has been stymied by a fear of failure?
6. Make a list of projects you need to complete which have been thwarted by procrastination.
7. Are you lazy? (To get an objective answer, ask a good friend.)
8. Have you become stagnant; are you in a rut?

4

Point Me in the Right Direction!
How to Set Goals

n this chapter we're going to talk about how to set goals. You'll need a pen and paper so you can write down your goals as you develop them because written goals are more likely to be achieved than goals that are mere thoughts. When we finish, you'll have a rough draft of several personalized planning charts.

Goal setting should permeate every area of our lives. If we disregard goal setting in any one area of life, that area will be neglected and will become anemic. If goal setting is beneficial in one area, it's good for all. Sometimes men and women will plan and set goals at the office—and see the benefits of doing so—but when they leave work and come home, they take off their planning hats. They have witnessed the advantage of having financial goals for their business but they have never adopted any personal financial goals. They don't realize that if goals work at the office, they will also work at home. So let's take a holistic approach to goal setting.

We'll begin by identifying the main areas of life in which goals should be set. Here's a suggested list. You may want to add other areas to your personal list, or you may want to subdivide some of these into smaller areas.

Spiritual
Financial
Marriage/Family
Physical
Educational
Personal/Social
Professional

Before we actually set goals in each of these areas, let me lay some groundwork and identify the scope of each area.

Spiritual

The development of your spiritual life should take precedence over all else, for what you are in your inner man will determine what you become in the outer man. We are tripartite in nature: we have a *body* (our physical body utilizing five senses), a *soul* (mind, will, and emotions), and a *spirit* (intuition, conscience, worship). While none should be neglected, our spirit should have priority. It's easy to spot someone who is preoccupied with the body—the guy who spends all his extra time pumping iron, or the girl who spends hours and dollars on making sure her makeup, hairstyle, suntan, clothes, and figure all conform to the latest standards in *Cosmopolitan* magazine. An overemphasis on soul development can result in an unhealthy obsession with intellectual development, self-discipline, psychology, or emotional extremes. Our spiritual lives must have precedence, for it is in this realm that we communicate with God and establish his will and precepts as the standards on which we will build our lives. Neglect of the inner man will lead to the demise of the outer man.

To mature spiritually, we have to work at it. It is possible to be born again and remain a baby Christian for years. I know Christians who have regularly attended church for thirty years, but they're no more mature today than they were thirty years ago. Why? Because they've never exerted the planned effort that growing up requires.

Before setting spiritual goals, you must settle one issue: are you sure you are born of God? If you died today, do you know that you would go to heaven? Do you have the assurance that Christ is in your life? These are important, foundational questions. Don't try to increase something that doesn't exist. Don't try to mature spiritually if you've never been born spiritually. That's like trying to build a house before you pour the foundation. Wrestle with this issue until you get it settled.

Then identify and embrace the major tenets of spiritual life and practice. Without hesitation we could name several: Bible study, prayer, praise, church life, witnessing. From a biblical, historical, and experiential perspective, these areas are important—yes, necessary—for spiritual growth. You must commit yourself to the study of God's Word if you're going to survive, much less thrive spiritually, and you need a plan, a system, a goal in this area. The same applies to prayer. It is necessary for your spiritual well-being, but if you don't plan to pray, you won't pray. If you don't have a "track to run on" relative to your prayer life, you'll be prayerless. It may be as simple as a list you pray through every morning, but you need a plan! The other areas—praise, church life, and witnessing—also need to be energized by plans.

Once these major tenets are accepted, they'll provide a framework for specific planning in the area of your spiritual life.

Financial

Before you draft some financial goals, you need a financial statement. You can get a financial statement form from any bank or lending institution, or you can write out your own, adapting the form at the end of this chapter. A financial statement will give an accurate picture of your financial condition. List all of your assets in one column and all your liabilities in another. Assets would include: cash, house, cars, property, jewelry, furniture, stocks, bonds, cash value of insurance policies—anything you own that has monetary value. (Be sure not to over-value your assets, particularly items such as furniture and jewelry. Don't record what you paid for them, but what you could *sell* them for.) Under liabilities list: mortgage amount, car loans, credit-card debt, or any other area for which you are financially responsible. When you subtract your total liabilities from your total assets, you have your net worth. Your financial statement should be updated yearly.

You also need an annual budget (a budget form is provided at the end of this chapter). Begin by conservatively estimating your yearly income. Then make a list of anticipated yearly expenses. This will include items like: house (payment, repair, and utilities), insurance, tithe to the Lord, medical, taxes, Social Security, food, clothes, entertainment, installment loans, savings, allowances, and school. A good way to anticipate expenses is to look at last year's check stubs. (You may also be surprised to see where you *did* spend your money!) Obviously, your total expenses should not exceed your income. If it does, you'll soon be in financial trouble. If you're married, both partners should be involved in developing the budget. It's also helpful to use a bookkeeping system that will give you a monthly update, comparing budgeted expenses to actual expenses. It will tell you if you're sticking to your budget or if you're getting off track.

A financial statement and a budget, will provide a solid framework for financial planning and goal setting. They should be reviewed and updated annually. Once they are established, other plans and goals can be integrated into the framework.

Marriage/Family

We have a great misconception in our society relative to becoming good spouses and parents. We think that saying *I do* at a church altar automatically makes one a good spouse, and we think that merely having a child immediately qualifies us as good parents. Wrong! It takes study, effort, and hard work, over a long period of time, to become a good husband or wife and father or mother.

For most of us, the only education we received on how to relate in marriage and how to raise kids was what we informally learned from our parents. This provided a good foundation for some, but what about parents who were raised in homes where mistakes were made? Regardless of whether our parents' example was good or bad, we all need to work on our family relationships. Again, a good relationship doesn't just "happen." It takes planned effort. If your family is a priority, you must set goals in this area.

Physical

With all the emphasis in recent years on diet, exercise, and physical fitness, it may seem unnecessary to elaborate on the importance of setting physical goals. But has the "feel better-live longer" wave hit you? Are you currently involved in caring for your body?

The truth is, your body *is* the temple of the Holy Spirit and should be treated as such. Furthermore, how you feel physically *will* affect how you fare mentally, emotionally, and spiritually. And finally, your body *is* the resting place for your soul and your spirit, and when your body ceases to function, your soul and spirit will have to go elsewhere.

Educational

An essential prerequisite to setting educational goals is to adapt the mind-set that our education is never complete. We should never stop learning. Our formal education, going full-time to a college or educational institution, may come to a climax, but the process of learning never ceases. If you don't keep actively learning, you'll regress. It's like pushing a wagon up a hill, if you let go and stop pushing, it will roll back down.

There are several reasons for this; one is—*we forget.* The attrition of our mind is unfortunate but real. How much content from a college course could you recall, six months after you finished the course? How much of last week's newspaper can you remember? What topics were covered on last week's "20/20" television show? We forget!

But we must also maintain a posture of constant learning because pertinent knowledge is always changing and the amount of pertinent knowledge is always increasing. You may have been "informed" politically two years ago, but you may be politically ignorant today if you haven't kept up. Fifteen years ago it was thought that red meat was an essential part of a healthy diet. If you've had your head in the sand, you probably still believe it. Pertinent knowledge changes daily, and we must constantly strive to keep current. But pertinent knowledge also increases. Our parents didn't have to be computer literate but we must. Nuclear energy was not an issue twenty years ago, but now you need to have an opinion. CPR was once only for the pros, but now every informed person is expected to be able to act competently if faced with a medical emergency. And what about your specific field of work? I wouldn't want to go to a doctor who was not apprised of recent medical advancements. I wouldn't even take my car to a mechanic who had not had updated training. Whatever field you work in, you must stay current in order to remain competent.

Besides all this, if you don't keep learning, you'll become a bore, and it's boring to be with a bore! Author Zig Ziglar says, "Happy, successful people don't *go* through life; they *grow* through life." So don't stop learning. Always have educational plans and goals.

Personal/Social

Personal plans and goals fall into two categories: personal improvement—that which will make you a more pleasing person; and personal desires—things that you have always wanted to do.

Perhaps you would like to dress more neatly or become a better conversationalist. These are areas of personal improvement. Developing these areas will make you feel better about yourself and help you to relate better with others. Or perhaps you have always wanted to travel to

Europe, or to play the piano. These desires are in your heart, and if you don't do them, you'll always regret it. These are personal desires and though they may be "self-oriented," they are important and real desires.

Social plans and goals involve how we relate to other people. God doesn't want any of us to be hermits, so we need to improve on our ability to relate to others. Have you slipped into a social cocoon? Do you only have one or two friends? Have you been living in the same house for years and still don't know your neighbors? Do you feel uncomfortable talking with others? Make some plans, set some goals, to get out of your social lethargy.

Professional

For those who work and are associated with a specific profession, it's advantageous to set professional goals.

The first step is to ask yourself: "Am I happy doing what I'm doing? Can I stay in this profession for the rest of my life and be satisfied? Am I a pharmacist by choice and desire, or did I just follow circumstantial currents?" If you respond hesitantly or negatively to these questions, you need to invest some time and serious thought into your choice of profession. It's never too late to change. Change may be difficult, but you only have one life to live; don't live it unfulfilled and bored.

But suppose you're in the right profession. How can you be better at what you do? Do you want to advance and if so, what will it take? How can you help your company or organization reach its goals? What can you do, besides what you've been doing, to increase productivity? What can you do to become a better employee or a better contributor to your profession? Your commitment to a few progressive plans can make a big difference in your professional career.

Three Goal-Setting Techniques

Now that we've identified the main areas in which goals should be made, let's set some goals. We'll use three different methods:

Satisfaction Assessment
Smorgasbord Technique
Wish-List Method

I suggest using three different methods because each one produces a different type of goal. The satisfaction-assessment technique will reveal areas of your life that need attention and will produce goals that are critical to your well-being. The smorgasbord technique is a mind stretcher because it forces you to consider alternatives which otherwise you would not have entertained. You'll discover some refreshing options and will probably want to latch on to a few of them. The wish-list method will help you vocalize those things you've always wanted to do but for one reason or another, never have.

Satisfaction Assessment

Using this goal-setting technique, first ask yourself the question, "How satisfied am I with each area (spiritual, financial, educational, and so on) of my life. Give yourself three possible choices:

very satisfied
satisfied, but there's room for improvement
dissatisfied

Next, complete this sentence for each area in which you are less than very satisfied, "I would be more satisfied if . . ."

In the area of marriage/family, the completed sentences might include:

. . . I spent more time with my kids.

. . . we went to church together as a family.

. . . I had better communication with my spouse.

. . . our sex life was more satisfying.

In the professional area, sample responses might read:

. . . I spent less time traveling.

. . . I could reduce the amount of paperwork that my job requires.

. . . I could move into a management position.

. . . I worked fewer hours.

Take enough time to work through each area. When you finish, you'll have a list of items which, if accomplished, would make your life more meaningful. The statements may not appear to be written down in ideal "goal form" (we'll discuss this later), but they will provide fertile ground from which goals can be harvested because they spring from needs and desires. You will be motivated to achieve these goals because you see them as a means of living a more fulfilled, satisfying life. These goals will have a lot of "pull" because they are a product of your own personal value system.

Smorgasbord Technique

Another approach to goal setting is the smorgasbord technique. You line up a large assortment of possible goals in each category, carefully consider each one, and see if any of them catch your eye. For instance, when considering goals listed under the "Financial" heading, you may be attracted to, "Start a college fund for your children." Perhaps it never occurred to you to plan for your children's higher education—but it's not a bad idea, is it? When you select goals in this manner, they are not as heartfelt as goals which come from a sense of need and desire, but the smorgasbord technique is effective because it makes you aware of possibilities which otherwise would have gone unnoticed.

Take a minute to scan through the following lists. Obviously, no one could do all of these activities, so don't bite off more than you can digest. Perhaps even limit yourself to one or two items per category.

Spiritual

Successfully complete the Evangelism Explosion Training Course.

Read through the Bible in one year.

Disciple four people.

Memorize one scripture per week.

Spend thirty minutes with God every day.

Read four biographies of great men of God.

Spend a week of vacation doing missions work.

Systematically listen to teaching tapes.

Teach a Sunday school class.

Lead three people to Christ during the next year.

Sing in the church choir.

Attend all corporate worship services of my local church.

Sign up for an hour in the prayer room.

Do volunteer work at the church one day a week.

Work in Vacation Bible School.

Participate in week-night visitation.

Be a sponsor at Youth Camp.

Make a financial commitment to the building fund.

Be a home cell group leader.

Serve as church usher.

Deal with resentment in my marriage.

Develop a forgiving spirit toward those who have offended me.

Financial

Develop a plan to become debt-free.

Start a college fund for my children.

Increase contribution to retirement fund.

Purchase a used car.

Pledge a designated amount to church building fund.

Tithe to the local church.

Buy an old house and fix it up for resale.

Teach part-time at the local junior college.

Buy new furniture.

Invest 10 percent of my annual income.

Save 10 percent of my annual income.

Keep better financial records.

Start a part-time business.

Abide by a yearly budget.

Attend a weekend financial seminar.

Control or eliminate all credit cards.

Complete work on family will.

Invest in mutual funds.

Marriage/Family

Attend a marriage-enrichment seminar.

Read three books this year on the marriage relationship.

Develop a better relationship with both in-laws.

Establish written communication with a distant relative.

Plan a yearly family reunion.

Buy bicycles for the family and ride together several times a week.

Develop specific guidelines relative to the discipline of our children.

Schedule a two-week family vacation.

Spend one night per week alone with my spouse.

Develop a family hobby.

House a foster child.

Set goals for our young children and help them attain the goals.

Enroll our children in a Christian school.

Start a garden.

Establish a family altar.

Have another child.

Devote Saturdays to family time.

Provide music lessons for my children.

Work to develop specific character traits in my children.

Establish a monthly planning day to discuss family members' schedules, goals, and so forth.

Physical

Participate in a regular exercise program.

Participate in a 10K run.

Learn to play tennis.

Lose a specific amount of weight.

Become more health-conscious in regard to diet.

Quit smoking.

Play racquetball twice a week.

Start jogging.

Drink less coffee.

Eat fewer desserts.

Do my own yardwork.

Exercise ten minutes every night.

Quit drinking.

Walk every evening.

Eat a nutritious breakfast.

Plant a flower garden.

Educational

Read two news-related periodicals a week.

Join a neighborhood book club.

Learn to use a personal computer.

Take a course at a nearby college.

Learn a hand skill.

Read one nonfiction book per month.

Begin work on a graduate degree.

Subscribe to the *New York Times.*

Attend night school.

Learn to raise orchids.

Watch educational TV shows.

Take music lessons.

Learn a foreign language.

Attend two conventions related to my profession.

Subscribe to and study two trade magazines.

Take a two-day course in some skill development.

Spend planned time with others in my profession.

Learn to type.

Personal/Social

Learn to sew.

Control the amount of time spent watching TV.

Develop two close friendships.

Dress more neatly.

Become more conversational.

Develop specific character traits (decisiveness, loyalty).

Eliminate specific bad habits (smoking, laziness).

Write a book.

Read one book every two weeks.

Buy and train a pet.

Start a stamp collection (or other hobby).

Communicate better with my spouse.

Travel to Europe.

Become a better public speaker.

Become a better listener.

Get to know my neighbors better.

Select two individuals or couples with which to develop a close relationship.

Attend a Bible study with people my own age and interest.

Become involved in a neighborhood association.

Start a monthly dinner club.

Become more friendly.

Volunteer one day a week at the hospital.

Join a softball league.

Professional

Apply for a transfer to another city.

Participate in more in-service training.

Look for another job.

Increase my management skills.

Delegate more responsibilities.

Don't bring any work home.

Apply for another job within the company.

Computerize all personal systems.

Spend more time with colleagues in my profession.

Hire a personal secretary.

Write an article for a trade journal.

Complete a master's degree in my field.

Ask for a raise in salary.

Wish-List Technique

This approach may remind you of the situation in the old movie where a man finds a friendly genie in a bottle which has been washed up on the beach, and the genie asks, "What do you wish, master?" I'm about to ask you a similar question, but unfortunately, you'll have to fulfill your own wishes.

Here's the question: "What have you always wanted to do, but haven't done?" Don't preface your answers with phrases like "Well, if I had the money." "If I had started younger." "If I had the time." Just write down four or five things you've always wanted to do but haven't done. I recently asked a few friends this question and these were some of their responses.

Travel to Europe.

Finish my college degree.

Compose and arrange music.

Be thin.

Write a book.

Hike the Appalachian Trail.

The Wish-List technique is effective because it helps identify strong, deep-rooted desires that have tenaciously remained through the years, desires that just will not go away. Interestingly, most people, when asked to list several "wish list" items, will not mention impractical, far-fetched fantasies like "Become a millionaire" or "Be president of I.B.M." or "Drive a Porsche." Usually the responses are quite simple and practical.

The three goal-setting techniques I've just discussed are best used in a formal "goal-setting session." Designate a period of time for the specific purpose of planning and goal-setting. I usually suggest setting aside several days a year to do formal planning. For example the last two weeks of December are slow weeks in my schedule so I do most of my planning then. For you, the end of the summer may be best. Choose a time when you can devote several days to relaxing, thinking, reading, praying, and Bible study. Don't force the plans to appear, just let them come.

But goals can also materialize when you're not really looking for them, so be on the alert. An idea may come while you're reading a magazine, listening to a lecture, folding the clothes, or playing with your hamster. Goal setting must be a constant, flexible, dynamic process. So when you've completed your annual planning time, don't think you're finished. If you go twelve months without updating and rethinking your plans, they'll die from neglect. Refer to your planning sheets every week.

It may take several years, but you'll eventually develop a planning "mind-set" that will make planning and goal setting an approach to life rather than a once a year activity. This mind-set will not eliminate the need for an annual planning session, it will just make planning more of a continuous function.

Before concluding this chapter, let me share some insights gleaned from nature which speak clearly to the issue of goal setting.

Laws of the Harvest

Every farmer will attest to the fact that there are certain "laws of the harvest" which are immutable. Three of these laws concern sowing and reaping. They also speak to the issue of life planning and goal setting.

1. *You always reap* what *you sow.*

The most obvious implication of this law is, if you don't sow, you won't reap. The farmer who is lazy during the planting season will also be playing dominoes during the harvest. It does take effort to sow, but without that effort there will be no produce. Many people are apprehensive about the future because they have been lazy or misdirected in the past. They have not put forth the time and effort required to plan for the future and to work their plans; therefore, they sadly await a barren future.

There is another inference in this first law of the harvest, it has to do with the *quality and type* of seeds sown and reaped. If you plant corn seeds, corn is what you'll get! Farmers are not surprised at the type of crop they harvest because they know what kind of seed they planted. The choice of fruit must be made before the sowing begins because once the seeds are planted, the harvest is unalterable. In one sense, we are consciously or unconsciously planting seeds every day. Daily activities, even attitudes, are not just fleeting, vanishing, here today-gone tomorrow entities—they are seeds. If you sow strife, discord, bitterness, and unforgiveness, you will reap the same. If you sow kindness, patience, and love, you'll reap the same. If you fill your days with meaningful, directed activities, you'll someday benefit from your investment.

2. *You reap later than you sow.*

We live in a "want it now" society. Every area of life has been victimized by the fast-food mentality. If something takes more than a few months to accomplish, we acquiesce to other, easier goals that have a shorter time requirement. But the best things in life don't come quickly. Quality relationships, a college education, a solid business, a stable church, professional skills—are all the result of long-term, directed investments.

The second law of the harvest simply encourages us to approach our daily work, not as an end to itself, but as an investment in the future. When the farmer plants his seeds, he's not frustrated at the lack of immediate results; he's content to know that someday his work will come to fruition.

That's why I encourage young people to consider the first thirty years of their lives as investment years. They should be years of learning, development, and planting. Many kids, on graduation from high school, begin working full-time because they want quick fruit. The prospects of immediately living in their own apartment, buying their own car, and being in the work force are just too tempting. Four years of college appears to them as a waste of time—a setback to their dreams of quick success. But alas, ten years later they're stuck; resigned to living off limited, available fruit for the rest of their lives. They don't have a harvest to look forward to.

A good dose of patience and more emphasis on the future would do all of us good.

3. *You reap* more *than you sow.*

This law of the harvest concerns the *amount* of return on investments. A farmer may plant a single kernel of corn but that small seed produces a large stalk with many ears of corn, each having hundreds of kernels. He reaps more than he sows.

Several years ago I led a friend to Christ and spent time discipling him. I invested some good time and effort into his life. I was planting seeds. My friend is now in full-time Christian service and has led many people to Christ and ministers to countless others. To the degree that I share in the joy of his victories, I am reaping much more than I sowed.

If other factors that influence the growing cycle are kept at optimum conditions (disease and insect control, adequate water, sunlight, and fertilizer), an abundant crop is the expected result of good farming. Likewise, if we cultivate and protect the seeds we have sown, we can expect a bountiful harvest.

Inherent in these three laws of the harvest is a "good news/bad news" scenario. The laws will either work in your favor or they'll work against you. If you sow bad seeds, you *will* reap the results, you will reap in the *future,* and you'll reap in *abundance.* That's the bad news. The good news is: if you sow good seeds, you will reap good results, in the future, and in abundance.

And that's the motivation behind strategic living. We must plan our days, weeks, and months in such a manner that we are constantly planting good seeds. Consider the seven areas we have discussed in this chapter (spiritual, financial, marriage/family, physical, educational, personal/social and professional), and start planting seeds in each area. Plant good seeds and then be patient. It may take several years for the fruit to come but it *will* come, and it will come in abundance.

Planning Charts

The following charts are very important. When you use them, theory becomes practice and the planning process is personalized. It may be more convenient to transfer the outline to your own calendar book or notebook and then fill in the blanks. Just be sure you do it.

The first chart asks you to write down policy statements for each area. A policy is a predetermined course of action which guides and determines present and future decisions. You might need to refer back to pp. 37–39.

In the spiritual area policies might include:

I will always be a faithful member of a local church.

I will always tithe.

I will always devote myself to daily Bible study and prayer.

I will refrain from all ungodly practices.

In the financial area policies might include:

I'll borrow money for a house but the monthly payment will not exceed 20 percent of my monthly income.

I'll use credit cards but only for budgeted items and the total balance due will be paid monthly.

I'll save 10 percent of my net income.

My family will own two cars. One must be paid for and the payment on the other will not exceed $250 per month.

You'll be surprised at how much strength policy statements have. When stated with sincerity, they become binding vows which demand accountability. They also provide general direction and long-range stability for all our goal setting.

You will actually write down your goals on the next three charts. They require that you consider the time dimension of each goal, that is, how long it will take to fulfill it. There are three charts, one each for long-range, medium-range, and short-range goals. These terms mean different things to different people but my definition is

short: 3 months–1 year

medium: 2–4 years

long: 5–15 years

For instance, when you're setting financial goals, the breakdown might look like this:

Long-range Goal   Retire with 70 percent of present annual income.
                        Eliminate house mortgage in fifteen years.

Medium-range Goal	Be debt free (except for house) in three years.
	Start a part-time consulting business.
Short-range Goal	Update my will.
	Purchase another car.

If you've been jotting down goals as we've worked through the three goal-setting techniques, it's simply a matter of placing what you already have in the proper spaces.

A financial statement form and a form that will help you develop a budget are also included.

Figure 3
Planning Charts

1. **Write policy statements for the following areas.**

   Spiritual

   1.

   2.

   3.

   Financial

   1.

   2.

   3.

   Marriage/Family

   1.

   2.

   3.

   Physical

   1.

   2.

   3.

   Educational

   1.

   2.

   3.

   Personal/Social

   1.

   2.

   3.

   Professional

   1.

   2.

   3.

2. Write long-range goals in the following areas. (These are goals you would like to accomplish in the next five to fifteen years.)

Spiritual

1.

2.

3.

Financial

1.

2.

3.

Marriage/Family

1.

2.

3.

Physical

1.

2.

3.

Educational

1.

2.

3.

Personal/Social

1.

2.

3.

Professional

1.

2.

3.

3. Write medium-range goals in the following areas. (these are goals you would like to accomplish in the next two to four years.)

Spiritual

1.

2.

3.

Financial

1.

2.

3.

Marriage/Family

1.

2.

3.

Physical

1.

2.

3.

Educational

1.

2.

3.

Personal/Social

1.

2.

3.

Professional

1.

2.

3.

4. Write short-range goals in the following areas. (These are goals you would like to accomplish in the next three months to one year.)

Spiritual

1.

2.

3.

Financial

1.

2.

3.

Marriage/Family

1.

2.

3.

Physical

1.

2.

3.

Educational

1.

2.

3.

Personal/Social

1.

2.

3.

Professional

1.

2.

3.

5. Complete this financial statement.

Financial Statement

WHAT YOU OWN		WHAT YOU OWE	
CASH:		**CURRENT BILLS:**	
Cash on hand	$	Rent	$
Checking accounts		Unilities	
Savings accounts		Charge accounts	
Money-market funds		Credit cards	
Life insurance cash value		Insurance premiums	
Money owed you		Alimony	
		Child support	
		Other bills	
MARKETABLE SECURITIES:			
Stocks	$		
Bonds		**TAXES:**	
Government securities		Federal	$
Mutual funds		State	
Other investments		Local	
PERSONAL PROPERTY:		Taxes on investments	
Automobiles	$	Other	
Household furnishings			
Art antiques, other collectibles			
Clothing, furs		**MORTGAGES:**	
Jewelry		Homes	$
Other possessions		Other Properties	
		DEBTS TO INDIVIDUALS:	
REAL ESTATE:			$
Homes	$		
Other Properties			
PENSION:			
Vested portion of company plan	$		
Vested benefits		**LOANS:**	
IRA		Auto	$
Keogh		Education	
LONG-TERM ASSETS:		Home improvement	
		Life insurance	
Equity in business	$	Other	
Life Insurance		**TOTAL: $**	
Annuities			
TOTAL: $		What you own minus what you owe equals your net worth: $	

6. Complete this budget form for the next twelve months.

Budget

INCOME		FIXED EXPENSES (cont'd)	
Salary	$	Loan or installment debt	
Bonus		repayment	$
Dividends		Other	
Interest			
Proceeds from the sale			
of securities			
Rental income		**TOTAL FIXED**	
Trust income		**EXPENSES**	**$**
Social security		**FLEXIBLE ESPENSES**	
Pension		Food/beverage	
Alimony		Clothing	
Child support		Laundry/cleaning	
Unemployment, Dis-		Personal care	
ability insurance		Entertainment	
Other income		Travel/vacation	
_____		Recreation	
_____		Gifts	
_____		Household help	
_____		Repairs	
_____		Home furnishings	
_____		Appliance purchases	
TOTAL INCOME:$		Gasoline	
FIXED EXPENSES		Communication	
Mortgage rent	$	Health care (doctors,	
Fuel		dentists, drugs)	
Electricity		Child care	
Telephone		Education	
Water		Gifts and donations	
Personal property taxes		Investments	
Realestate taxes		Savings	
Homeowner insurance		Personal Allowance	
premium		Other	
Automobile insurance		_____	
premium		_____	
Medical disability Ins-		_____	
urance premium		**TOTAL FLEXIBLE**	
Life insuracne premium		**EXPENSES**	**$**
Automobile loan		**TOTAL EXPENSES**	**$**

5

Do It!
How to Accomplish Goals

A forest would not exist unless each tree had started out as a seed, but a sack of seeds does not make a forest. Making ideas work is as important as having the ideas in the first place.

EDWARD DE BONO

Many God-inspired, heart-warming dreams and plans have succumbed to atrophy because they never made it to the implementation stage. A plan, regardless of how appropriate, proper, or noble it is, *remains* a plan unless action is taken. Knowing what you want to accomplish and having the skills to do it, is not enough.

You must plan to plan, but you must also plan to act. How often have you participated in a planning meeting in which many wonderful plans were generated and agreed upon, but then the meeting was dismissed and everyone went to lunch, thinking the job was complete. Unless

109

someone took the initiative to go back to the drawing board and plan a strategy to implement the plans, the plans probably went into default. The planning process is not complete until we have planned to *act*.

In the last chapter we discussed how to develop plans. I hope you completed the worksheets and now have a list of things you want to see accomplished in your life. In this chapter we're going to deal with how to accomplish those plans.

Three Important Steps

There are three steps to accomplishing a goal. I tried to design an acrostic that would help us remember the three steps, so how about: I.R.S. (a term everyone remembers at least once a year).

> **I**dentify
> **R**educe
> **S**chedule

First we must *Identify* what it will take to accomplish the goal.

Some goals are so simple, they can be reached in one step. If the oil in your car needs changing, just drive down to the service station and get it done. Or if you need to make a dental appointment, one phone call is all it takes. But most goals are more complex than that and require a series of actions, or subgoals. For instance, if you want to have a dinner party for some friends, there are numerous tasks which must be considered. You must: decide on a guest list, send invitations, plan the menu, buy the supplies, clean the house, prepare the meal, clean up afterwards. The one goal of having a dinner party is actually a summation of many subgoals. If you consider a more complex, long-range goal, such as earning a college degree, you can imagine the innumerable tasks which would be necessary to reach the main goal.

So once we've established a goal, the first step toward implementation is to identify the goal's component parts. We're looking for three to five subplans, which, when accomplished, will be the sum total of the main goal. In formula form it would look like this: $A+B+C+D=Goal$. If A, B, C, and D are accomplished, the goal will be realized.

The next step is to *Reduce* the major subplans into smaller units of work, and continue to reduce the subplans until you have a list of manageable activities that can be completed in less than one hour or at one setting. It's like diagraming a sentence, the sum of all the parts equals the whole. The formula now looks like figure 2.

Figure 2

A.	+	B.	+	C.	+	D.	= Goal
1.		1.		1.		1.	
2.		2.		a.		2.	
3.		a.		b.		3.	
		b.		2.		4.	
		c.		a.		5.	
				b.			
				c.			

Let's apply this formula to our goal of having a dinner party. The diagram would look like this:

Goal—Have a dinner party for friends.
Subplans and units of work.
  A. Decide on a guest list (confer with husband).
  B. Send invitations.
    1. buy invitations and stamps.
    2. get current addresses.
    3. write out invitations and mail.

   C. Plan the menu.
      1. look through several cookbooks.
      2. make a list of supplies needed.
      3. experiment, if necessary, with a recipe.
   D. Buy the supplies.
      1. prepare a master list.
      2. go through coupon box.
      3. shop for groceries.
      4. pick up flower arrangement.
   E. Clean the house.
   F. Prepare the meal.
      1. cook some items the night before.
      2. prepare hors d'oeuvres.
      3. cook the main entree.
   G. Clean up after the dinner.

You'll notice that three of the subplans (A, E, & G.) are not broken down any further because they are simple tasks.

The final step is to *schedule* these subplans and units of work into your daily or weekly schedule. For instance, schedule B1 to be done Friday, 9:00-10:00 A.M.; B2 on Sunday, 2:00-3:00 P.M., and so forth until all the subunits are scheduled. Then it will just be a matter of time until the goal is accomplished. If this looks easy, it should—because it is!

Stated another way: to accomplish a goal you must answer three questions: *What, How,* and *When.*

   What do I want to do? (Set your goal.)

   How do I do it? (Identify and reduce.)

   When am I going to do it? (Schedule.)

Let's look at the I.R.S. plan in more detail, along with another example.

One of our family goals last year was to design and build a new house. So the answer to the *what* question was—*build a house.*

At this stage, it's very important to know for sure that the goal is valid and that it will be worth the cost required. Before you move to the *identify* and *reduce* stage, and for sure before you get to the *schedule* stage, make sure the goal is really what you want. Some people climb a tall ladder, only to discover that it's leaning against the wrong wall. So far no energy or assets have been expended. You can ditch the effort at this point, and you will not have lost anything. It's like starting out on a long journey—make sure you're pointed in the right direction before you take the first step! A little research is usually necessary to adequately "count the cost" and to make sure the goal is worthwhile. Perform a cost/benefit analysis on the project. Will the benefit derived from the project justify the cost it takes to complete it?

Testing the Feasibility

Whenever I set a goal that is going to require a lot of resources (time, money, effort), I usually filter it through several "tests" to make sure the goal is feasible and is indeed something I want to pursue.

The first test is the *test of time*. I let the goal simmer in my mind for months before I take any action. It's amazing how many flashing thoughts and impulsive ideas will slowly fade away with time. Very few important decisions require immediate response. If a goal is right for you, its pull will not diminish in time but will increase.

It's also helpful to *consult people who have already accomplished what you're thinking about doing*. Most successful people want to help others. They are eager to share their path to success and the obstacles they had to overcome to get there. If you're thinking about starting a restaurant, building a house, buying a boat, or attending a certain college, visit with those who have already done it.

Another test involves *seeking the counsel of godly friends, particularly those who don't have any first-hand experience in the area you're considering.* Sometimes friends can give better, objective advice because they're *not* involved than those who have biased opinions based on their own success. Friends, particularly those who are our elders, can often see the "big picture" more clearly than we can. They should be consulted.

For example, several years ago I had a "bright idea" which, under close investigation, fizzled out. I considered starting a music publishing company that would specialize in printing sacred, choral classics. A wonderful goal— I thought. I let it simmer in my mind for a while, and it was still on the front burner, so I decided to pursue it further. The next step was to ask the advice of a friend who was in the music-publishing business. Our twenty-minute conversation put a permanent freeze on the idea. He informed me that in recent years three large music-publishing companies had gobbled up all the small independent firms, making survival almost impossible for a small operation. Also, I was thinking that an initial mailing list of twenty-five hundred would be sufficient but he informed me that a list of fifty thousand would be barely adequate. After our conversation I quickly and forever abandoned the goal. Had I not waited and done a little research, many resources would have been expended toward a project that was doomed from the beginning.

Following Through on the House Project

Back to the house project. My wife and I had prayed about building a house for several years, and we got a green light at every checkpoint. We had solidified in our hearts a goal which we knew God was in favor of: build a house.

The next step was to *Identify* what it would take to accomplish the goal. We broke the major goal into these subplans.

Goal: Build a house.
Subplans
A. Sell our present house.
B. Find a lot.
C. Select/design house plans.
D. Secure a builder.
E. Make necessary selections.
F. Supervise construction.
G. Arrange for financing: interim and permanent.
H. Move.

We're now beginning to answer the *how* question. If *what* we want to do is build a house, *how* are we going to do it?

It's important that the list of subplans be complete. Does the sum of these parts equal the whole, or have we left something out? Can every minute detail be placed under one of these subplans? If you omit an essential area, the goal will not be achieved. Additional research may be necessary to ensure that your subplans are complete. We had built a house before so we were aware of what it would involve. Had we been uninitiated, a visit with someone who had recently built a house, a conversation with the city's home-builders' association, or a trip to the library would have provided the necessary input.

Also at this stage, it's good to requestion the entire project. In lieu of knowing more detail about what the project involves, do I still want to do it? Do I have the resources to complete the task?

Once subplans have been identified the next task is to *Reduce* each subplan into small units of activity. Keep reducing until you write down an activity that can be done in less than one hour or at one sitting.

In our house-building saga, it looked like this for one of the subplans:

Goal—Build a house.
Subplan A—Sell our present house.
Reduced activities:
1. Prepare the house for marketing.
   a. to paint the exterior.
         select and buy paint.
         prepare surface.
         paint.
   b. to plant new shrubs.
         purchase plants.
         remove old shrubs.
         plant new shrubs.
   c. to replace dishwasher.
         purchase new unit.
         arrange for installation.
   d. clean house every four days.
2. Get an appraisal.
   a. arrange for a professional appraisal.
   b. get marketing appraisal from real-estate agent.
3. Select a real-estate firm and agent and market the house.
   a. interview several agents.
   b. talk to neighbors who have recently bought/sold a house.
   c. get facts regarding different agencies from the Board of Realtors.
   d. sign contract.
   e. design marketing strategy.

It's at this stage that large, seemingly impossible goals, are broken down into small manageable parts. The reason some people never accomplish "big things" in life is that they never reduce them to small units that can be handled. *The Guinness Book of World Records* records the true story of a man who ate a bicycle. That's right—he ate an entire bicycle, tires and all! But he didn't eat it all at once. Over a period of 15 days, from March 17 to April 2, 1977, Michel Lotito of Grenoble, France, melted the parts into small swallowable units and consumed every piece. Why anyone would want to eat a bicycle, I'll never know, but the anecdote does speak to the fact that just about anything can be done if it's broken down into small manageable parts. Or, as the adage states: "Life by the yard is apt to be hard; life by the inch is more of a cinch."

Be a "Detail Person"

When we talk about a "detail person," we're referring to a person who can see a large project dissected into hundreds and sometimes thousands of small details—and recognize the importance of these details. Everyone needs a good dose of this serum. "But I'm a manager; I just deal with the big picture," you may say. What about your personal life and your family life? Do you delegate everything in those areas? (I hope not!) Besides, being a detail person does not make you less of an administrator—it makes you a better one.

Regardless of how big a project is, it can and must be broken down into small units of work which can be scheduled and performed. One of the most challenging projects of this century was posed by President John F. Kennedy when he said, "I believe that this nation should commit itself to achieving the goal, before the decade is out, of landing a man on the moon and returning him safely to earth."

The goal was very simple: an American foot contacting lunar soil. But that grandiose goal had to be broken down into thousands of subplans, and the subplans were further diagramed into millions of small activities. A lab technician in Silicon Valley spent an hour of her day testing the heat resistance of a tiny computer chip. A machinist in Baytown, Texas, worked for several hours on a dal-rod. A physicist at some university invested week after week in studying the effect of a weightless atmosphere on certain types of clothing. All these, and countless other activities, were parts of a goal—to put a man on the moon.

What are some things that you've always wanted to do, but they seemed formidable and impossible: finish a college degree, write a book, start your own business, hunt wild game in Africa, learn how to sew, play an instrument? If you're sure it's right for you, and it's worth the cost, take out a piece of paper and at the top write down your goal and then, to the best of your knowledge, break down the goal into smaller subplans. Then dissect the subplans into small units of work.

Scheduling

Now you're ready for the next step. *Schedule* these units of work into your daily or weekly schedule. At this point dreams materialize into reality. In colloquial terms this is where the "rubber meets the road." Up to this point, the goal is only on paper—no action has been taken. But now things need to happen in the physical world that must be scheduled and performed. At this stage the goal will produce meaningful action.

One of my subplans for building the house was "sell

our present house" and under that were four major units of work which were further divided into small units of activity. It's now simply a matter of putting these small units of work into my schedule book and then performing the work. My first week might look like this:

Monday
12:00-1:00   Go to paint store to select and purchase paint.
5:00-7:00   Shop for new dishwasher.

Tuesday
10:00   Call Board of Realtors and Appraiser's Office.

Wednesday
12:00-1:00   Purchase new shrubs.
3:00   Wife home for dishwasher installation and appraiser.
5:00-8:00   Remove old shrubs and plant new ones.
9:00   Call some high school boys to help paint on Saturday.

Thursday
Day is all full.

Friday
10:00   Meet with prospective real-estate agent.
3:00   Call neighbor who recently sold his house.

Saturday
8:00-12:00   Prepare exterior surface for paint.
1:00-5:00   Paint exterior surface with hired help.

Within a month (depending on the market) subplan A "sell our present house" could feasibly be completed. Simultaneously, work units from other subplans could be scheduled, and in time, we're living in a new house.

Scheduling answers the last of the three questions, which must be answered if a goal is to be accomplished.

The answer to the *what* question was build a house. The answer to the *how* question was a series of subplans and activities. The answer to the *when* question impacted my daily schedule. After setting a goal, you *identify, reduce,* and *schedule.* Because scheduling is such an important aspect of this process, the next chapter will treat it in detail.

This I.R.S. system provides the key to living a productive life. If you work at it, it's possible to spend the majority of every day working on meaningful subplans and activities. If you perform just four or five meaningful activities a day (after all, we have about sixteen nonsleeping hours per day), that would accumulate to twenty-eight to thirty-five in one week. Productive weeks produce productive months, which lead to productive lives. Unfortunately, if you ask most people what their plans are for the next day, they reply, "I'm going to the office and just do whatever needs to be done." There's a lot of wasted time and misdirected energy in that mode of operation. It's much better to know what you're going to do before you get to the office.

Give yourself a quick productivity check by writing down the things you have done in the past two days that contributed to a larger goal that is yet to be achieved. I'm not referring to "maintenance items" like eating, taking the kids to school, doing the laundry, and putting gas in the car. These items need to be scheduled too, but have you done anything in the past two days that functioned as pieces of a large puzzle? You don't have to adopt a stressful, unrelenting lifestyle to be productive; just a few meaningful, directed activities per day will soon add up to major accomplishments.

Another benefit of the I.R.S. system is that it helps us gain control of our lives. If a friend calls and asks, "What are you doing Monday evening?" if you have nothing planned, you'll probably end up doing what he wants to do. However, if you've already planned to go shopping for a dishwasher because you want to sell your house, he'll probably end up going with you.

An important aspect of *Doing It* involves the constant monitoring of your progress, or lack of it, toward your goals. Goals and plans must continually be fine-tuned. Very seldom can you "set up" a strategy and then switch to automatic pilot, there are just too many unknown factors and changing conditions. Many fine aspirations have died in midlife because they were neglected, there was no follow-through after initiation.

Keep a Journal

One good way to monitor the plans and goals you're working on is to keep a journal. At the top of a blank sheet of paper, write down the plan along with the reduced activities necessary to fulfill the plan. Continually refer to the sheet, checking off items which have been completed, making notes about difficulties encountered and changing subplans. Having a visual aid helps you to see the project clearly and objectively.

A weekly planning session can also provide an opportunity for monitoring. Designate a specific hour of the week, perhaps Sunday evening, as your weekly planning/evaluation time. Spend part of the time planning for the upcoming week but also use the hour to monitor the progress you've made toward long-range plans.

Strategic living encourages the patient, progressive realization of worthwhile goals. It runs cross-grain to a "get-it-quick, want-it-now" approach. We should always plan for consistent, gradual improvement. We should be satisfied with small, directed steps instead of spectacular leaps. Everything worthwhile in life is achieved through the persistent accumulation of small tasks.

This commitment to gradual progress is seen in the life of Wernher von Braun, the German scientist who followed a steady course of scientific pursuit toward the development of rocketry. David Swartz summarized (Swartz 1983, 204) his tenacious aspiration.

> Consider the persistent patience Wernher von Braun used in developing rockets that paved the way for space exploration and satellite communications. In the 1920's, as a teenager, Von Braun dreamed of man someday exploring the moon. In those days, the idea of human beings venturing into space was pure fantasy. But that didn't stop Von Braun. In the 1930's, the Germans saw the potential of rockets as a weapon and Von Braun was put to work building rockets. Using missiles for war was not the use Von Braun had in mind for them, and in 1944 he was put in jail. Soon his talents were recognized as vital to the German war effort and he was released. He was told to put deadly rockets into space against England.
>
> After World War II, Von Braun directed the team that put the first American satellite, Explorer I, into orbit. His team also launched the flight of our first astronaut, Alan Shepard, in 1961. Von Braun played the largest role of any person in the first moon landing. No one else did so much to introduce the world to the space age. And he did it through enormous persistency. Failures of his experiments outnumbered successes by ten to one. But he knew his ultimate objective was worthy, that it was feasible, and so he persisted. His persistent patience will have an impact on mankind forever.

When to Give Up a Goal

Before concluding this chapter, one more issue needs to be addressed—when do you give up on a goal? When does determination turn to obstinacy; how long should you continue pursuing a plan when it appears doomed to failure?

I hesitate to even mention this topic because more times than not, we give up too easily and too quickly. Usually the problem is that we lack determination, not that we have too much of it! Nevertheless there are times when the most prudent thing to do is to abandon a plan or goal, even if you've invested considerable resources toward its accomplishment. Or, as de Bono states, "Salt on food is good up to a point, beyond which it ruins the food. Courage is good up to a point, beyond that point it becomes foolhardiness. Persistence is good up to a point, beyond which it becomes stubbornness." What are the conditions under which goals and plans should be abandoned? There are several.

Some goals have a very narrow definition of success, it's all or nothing, do or die. For instance, there's no value in attending medical school if you don't pass the final medical exam. Or, if you're involved in a political election because your goal is to be mayor of your city but early polls indicate that you only have 2 percent of the votes, you'd better drop out and invest your energies elsewhere. In these goals, getting close is not good enough. If you don't make it past the final hurdle, all is lost.

Contrast these goals, however, with the type that provide a measure of success, even if partially reached. If you set a goal to lose 40 pounds, but only lose 35 pounds, you're not going to complain. If a person sets a goal to earn a million dollars in ten years but only earns $950,000, no one will consider him a failure. In these goals, every increment of progress is regarded as success, and if the ultimate goal is not reached, all is not lost.

But if you're working on a "do or die" goal and you realize you're probably not going to make it, it might be wise to quit. I once read about a chess game played by two world-class champions. The winner of four out of seven games would win the tournament. After only five moves in game one, one of the players forfeited the game. When asked by a reporter why he gave up so quickly, he replied: "Based upon the first five moves of the game, I looked ahead and could see that I would be checkmated on the twenty-fifth play. There was no reason to continue the game." That's not weakness—that's wisdom.

Another valid reason to abandon a goal is if you realize that the results attained by reaching the goal are not what you want. In this scenario, the chances of your reaching the goal are good; you're just not interested in the final results. Or, as I mentioned earlier, you may climb to the top of the ladder only to realize that the ladder is leaning against the wrong wall. I have a friend who just completed his first year of law school and then dropped out. It's not because he couldn't finish law school; he's a fine student. He just realized that he doesn't want to be a lawyer. He wants to be a minister, so he's going to enroll in seminary.

The goal-setting process should always be tempered with realism and flexibility. With well-thought-out goals, very few should have to be abandoned but inevitably, some of our files must go to the trash can. Don't have such a tenacious grip on the boat that if it begins to sink, you go down with it.

Conclusion

The I. R. S. system will help you accomplish your goals. It will eliminate the separation of muscle power from brain power, it will link execution to strategy. D. L. Moody, pastor and church leader, was always inclined toward action. He once approached a leader in his church about a

clever promotional idea and asked, "What do you think?"
"We've been aimin' to do that for years," the layman replied. "Well, then," Moody replied, "don't you think it's
time to fire?"

What are some of the goals and plans you've been aim-
ing at? It's time to fire!

Discussion Questions

1. Why do some of your plans never come to fruition?
   What must be done to ensure that the plans you wrote
   down at the end of chapter 4 are fulfilled?
2. Before you begin to pursue a goal, do you spend adequate time investigating its validity?
3. Do you plan each day's activities or do you just "do
   whatever needs to be done"?
4. On separate sheets of paper write down all the short-
   range goals you established at the end of chapter 4.
   There were seven different categories, and if you wrote
   down two goals for each category, you have fourteen
   goals so use fourteen sheets of paper. Take each goal
   through the I.R.S. plan. I know this is going to take
   a long time but if you don't Identify, Reduce, and
   Schedule, your goals will never materialize. Remember, it's not enough just to plan, you must move beyond
   the planning stage and implement what you want to
   do.

6

Do It When?
Scheduling

We have left undone
    those things
        which we ought to have done . . .
                The Book of Common Prayer, 1552

Whenever I teach a seminar on Strategic Living, I tell my audience at the beginning of our time together, that the most important session of the entire seminar is the session on scheduling. "Don't miss it!", I admonish them. For without a good, workable knowledge of how to schedule, our best laid plans and intentions will go to naught. It's not enough to know *what* you want to do, or even *how* to do it. Even if you have the capability and motivation to do a task, without proper scheduling, you'll end up making the same confession as this sixteenth-century author of the Book of Common Prayer. Scheduling is the most vital link in the planning process.

Here are five steps which, if utilized, will help you gain control of your life. Your daily productivity will increase and you'll begin to see those large, formidable goals come to fruition.

1. Commit yourself to some type of datebook.

A datebook is simply a calendar book that has enough room for some notes next to each day's space. I use the Day-Timer System. Unless you're already working with another type of notebook that you really enjoy, I would encourage you to at least investigate their system. It is available in various formats and sizes and is relatively inexpensive. For a free catalog, write: Day-Timers, Allentown, Pa. 18001.

Regardless of which system you use, you must limit yourself to just one datebook. Some executives have one or two planning calendars at the office and another one at home that they use for personal planning and scheduling. Using multiple datebooks is counterproductive; use one exclusively. This one datebook should become "Command Central," coordinating and unifying all your efforts.

It is also important that you keep your datebook with you at all times. "Don't leave home without it!" is good advice here too. That's why many people use the pocket-size Day-Timer. It is easy to carry around. I prefer the $8 \frac{1}{2} \times 11$, three-ring-binder, and very seldom is it out of my reach. Get into the habit of carrying it with you wherever you go.

2. In your datebook, keep a copy of your plans and goals, a "catch-all list," and all "project work sheets."

Plans and goals

Using the three goal-setting techniques discussed in chapter 4, you should now have a list of plans and goals for all the major areas of your life. Each goal should also have been reduced into smaller units of work that can be performed in one hour or at one sitting. *These goals must be kept in your datebook!* If you put them in a filing cabinet, they'll never be accomplished. "Out of sight, out of mind," will certainly prevail. Plans must be constantly monitored, and the best way to do that is to keep them easily accessible. (This is one advantage of the three-ring binder system; numerous sheets and dividers can be added and subtracted from the datebook, which gives most control over its content.) A sample list of plans and goals is shown on page 130.

Catch-all list

Suppose you're sitting in your office and you remember that you haven't made your monthly car payment. You need to write yourself a reminder note so you won't forget again, but where do you write the note? Write it on your catch-all list. Later in the morning you think about the airline reservations you need to make for your vacation. Again, write yourself a note on the catch-all list. A friend takes you to lunch and you need to write him a thank-you note. Just open your datebook to your catch-all list and write, "John-thank you note."

A catch-all list is simply a continuous listing of various activities you need to perform. They are not listed by priority or importance. You may have an entry such as "fertilize the marigolds" followed by "call Chicago about contract." "Pick up the laundry," may be preceeded by "plan conference for five years from now." Regardless of how important or trivial items may be, write all of them on the catch-all list. The list will always contain items which surface during day-to-day living, activities that would probably never show up on a plan or goal sheet.

Sample List of Goals and Plans

Marriage/Family

Medium-Range Goals and Plans

1. Take one, two-week vacation this year.
   a. Talk to family about where they want to go.
   b. Allocate $200.00 per month from the budget for the trip.
   c. Make appropriage arrangements for transportation and lodging.
   d. Arrange to be gone from work.
   e. Make arrangements for someone to watch the house.

2. Develop a family hobby—riding bikes.
   a. Purchase bikes (get money out of savings).
   b. Set aside one evening a week to go riding.
   c. Develop different bike trails.

3. Have a "date" with my wife once a week—without the kids.
   a. Discuss with Mary which night is best.
   b. Arrange for baby-sitter.
   c. Allocate enough money for the evening.
   d. Put thise dates on my datebook.

4. Encourage the kids to read more books.
   a. Take them to the library every two weeks.
   b. Design an award system to motivate them.
   c. Teach them how to write a book report.
   d. Set aside one afternoon a week for reading time.

5. Control the amount of TV the family watches.
   a. Look through the TV guide on Sunday and decide which programs we want to see for the whole week.
   b. program the VCR to record these programs.
   c. Schedula a "TV night" to watch the tapes.

6. Attend a marriage seminar with my wife.
   a. Determine which dates a seminar is being offered.
   b. Schedule a baby-sitter for that weekend.
   c. Mark off the seminar dates in our datebook.

The important consideration here is: *Don't randomly place any item in your daily journal—put it on your catch-all list.* For instance, if it's July 14, and you remember that you need to write your mother-in-law a letter, don't put the note "write mother-in-law" under July 14, put it on your catch-all list. For one thing, we don't want to clutter up the space reserved for daily activities, and also, when various things come to mind, that's usually not the best time to properly prioritize them and schedule them in an efficient manner.

A sample catch-all list is shown on page 132.

Project Work Sheets

Periodically, you'll have an entry on your catch-all list that is not a simple activity (one that can be done in one hour or at one sitting). As we learned in chapter 4, these activities need to be broken down into smaller units of work. "Write mother-in-law" and "fertilize the marigolds" are simple activities. They only need to be scheduled in your datebook. However, "plan conference for five years from now" needs to be broken down—you need to write out a *project worksheet*. For this particular project, the worksheet might look like the sample on page 133.

You should keep in your datebook, copies of all your project worksheets. You may have as many as ten or fifteen projects that you're working on simultaneously. When you complete a project, take out the worksheet and put it in a file. Project worksheets are helpful because they allow you to see all the related elements that need to be scheduled and completed.

The first step to successful scheduling is to commit yourself to one datebook and always have the datebook available. The second key to successful scheduling is to keep in your datebook, three lists: a copy of your plans

Notes and Memos

item no.	Number each item

Notes and Memos

item no.	Number each item

and goals, a catch-all list, and all your project worksheets. The next step is to:

3. Schedule your plans and goals, items on your catch-all list, and items on your project worksheets based on:

        1. Priority
        2. Economy of time and effort
        3. Logical progression

First, let's consider—priority.

Priority

We prioritize according to two criteria: importance and urgency. We have to consider both. Usually, important things are not urgent, so if we prioritize based only on what's urgent, we'll not accomplish the important things in life. For instance, it's important to read. If we want to grow intellectually, keep up on current issues, and stimulate our minds, we need to read. But reading a book will never be an "urgent" matter. If our days are consumed with attending to pressing issues, we'll never read. Likewise, earning a college degree is important, but it will never present itself as an emergency issue demanding immediate attention. Usually, medium- and long-range goals never have an urgency about them because they don't require immediate action. So when we prioritize, we must primarily consider the question, "What is important?"

But there are also urgent matters. Webster defines *urgent* as: "calling for immediate attention." No matter how hard you try to avoid emergency situations, things do come up that have to be addressed quickly. For instance, one night several weeks ago, I had my next day planned

Sample Worksheet

Conference 199__

A. Select conference site.
1. Contact various chambers of commerce.
2. Contact hotels in different cities.
3. Informally poll those who will attend the conference as to their preference of location.

B. Solidify conference speakers.
1. Prioritize speaker preference.
2. Contact speakers.
3. Solidify topics.

C. Solidify dates for conference.
1. Find out dates of other conferences.
2. Coordinate with guest speakers' schedule.
3. Coordinate with convention center.
4. Solidify daily schedule.

D. Advertise conference.
1. Design conference logo and slogan.
2. Solidify use of radio and TV.
3. Prepare all printed materials.
4. Prepare mailing list.

(Many of these items need to be broken down further, but to save space, I'll leave it in this form.)

out from morning to night. My datebook was filled with "important" projects. However, about 11:00 P.M., my third molar, top left-hand side, started aching. The situation regressed to the point that I stayed up all night long, nursing a bad root canal. The next morning, needless to say, I defaulted on my well planned, important schedule in favor of an urgent matter—get to the dentist as quickly as possible.

So I don't view urgent matters as some deadly virus

which attacks the daily schedule. I disagree with the negative connotation of the phrase "the tyranny of the urgent." Urgent matters do surface, and most of them are legitimate. (Distractions are quite different, I'll discuss them in the next chapter.) If you have a flat tire on the way to work, that becomes an urgent matter. If your daughter gets sick in school and you have to go pick her up, that's an urgent matter. It's just a matter of balancing the urgent with the important.

Here are some guidelines to help you prioritize:

Prioritize according to importance

When you're looking over your plans and goals, your catch-all list, and your project worksheets, ask yourself these questions:

Which tasks are the most important, and, if performed, will produce the most satisfying results?

Which plans are important but not critical, and, if not accomplished, will not have significantly negative results?

Which items could possibly be neglected, or at least postponed?

Prioritize according to urgency

When you're about to schedule your next day's activities, consider these variables:

How much time do I need to complete a particular task, and what is the deadline?

If this task is not done quickly, what will the penalties be?

Again, the key to prioritizing is balance. Learn to juggle urgent matters while keeping your focus on important ones.

The following will illustrate the difference between important issues and urgent ones and how they should be considered in the scheduling process.

You're a high school basketball coach and you've just received word that your team has been invited to play in a tournament in another state. Your request to participate in the tournament had previously been denied, but a team dropped out and they chose your team as the replacement. There's only one hitch—the tournament starts in two weeks.

The first thing you need to do is make a list of all tasks that must be done if the project is to be successful. The list would probably include these items:

Ask the principal for permission to take the team out of school for five days.

Arrange for transportation.

Contact the players and their parents to see how many can participate.

Make hotel reservations.

Buy new uniforms.

Find a substitute teacher for your classes.

Call the tournament organizer about your response.

Arrange for the team to have a free day at an amusement park that's in the city you'll be visiting.

Write out a detailed itinerary of the trip.

Schedule several extra practices.

Solicit sponsors for the trip.

Get permission slips from the parents.

Notify other teachers of the players who will be absent.

Get game films of the teams you'll be competing against.

Next, prioritize all the tasks according to importance:

Most Important

Ask the school principal for permission to make the trip.

Contact the players/parents and see who can participate.

Make hotel reservations.

Arrange for transportation.

Call the tournament organizer about your response.

Get permission slips from the parents.

Important, But Not Critical

Find a substitute teacher.

Write out a detailed itinerary of the trip.

Solicit sponsors for the trip.

Notify other teachers of the team's absence.

Optional

Schedule several extra practices.

Get game films of the competing teams.

Make arrangements to visit the amusement park.

Buy new uniforms.

We now have all the tasks prioritized according to importance. Items listed under "most important" are tasks which must be completed or the project will not be successful. For instance, until you get permission from the principal to make the trip, all other tasks are negligible. Likewise, until you find out which players can participate, there's not much use in pursuing other tasks. The items listed under "important but not critical" are indeed important but not as important as the first category. As we move from the "most important" tasks to the "optional" tasks, it's easy to see that there are some items that must be done if the trip is to be successful and there are others which could be neglected without jeopardizing the trip. For instance, the team could play without new uniforms, but they can't play unless you get them there (transportation).

The next thing we need to do is prioritize all tasks according to urgency. Remember, when considering the urgency of each task, we need to ask, "How much time will it take me to complete a task and what is the deadline?" and, "If this task is not done quickly, what will it cost me?"

First, let's prioritize (according to urgency) the items listed under "Most Important."

It's important to contact the principal about the trip, but it's not necessarily urgent because it can be done very quickly (it will not take long to complete this task), just call his office and arrange for a time to meet. Getting a response from the players would be considered an urgent matter because of the length of time it takes to complete the tasks and the deadline you have to work with. You have to communicate information about the trip to the players, and then they have to talk to their parents. Making hotel arrangements is an urgent matter. If you wait too long, all rooms may be taken. Relative to transportation, you know the athletic department's buses are available, so that's not an urgent concern. The organizer of the tournament has given you five days to respond, so your response can wait. Getting permission slips from the players is important but it could wait till the last minute, since you're getting a verbal response from the parents immediately.

So the same list, prioritized according to urgency, would look like this:

1. Contact the players/parents and see who can participate.
2. Call about hotel arrangements.
3. Ask principal for permission.
4. Call tournament organizer.
5. Solidify transportation.
6. Get permission slips from parents.

Next, we'll prioritize (according to urgency) the items under "Important, But Not Critical."

The most urgent item on this list is to recruit some sponsors for the trip. Whoever goes on the trip needs to make arrangements to miss work or be away from their house for five days. They need as much advance notice as possible. The next most urgent thing is to find a substitute teacher so lesson plans can be prepared, and so forth. It is important to notify the teachers regarding which students will be going on the trip, but this could probably be postponed several days. Writing a detailed itinerary of the trip could be done the day before you leave.

So the same list, prioritized according to urgency, would look like this:

1. Solicit sponsors for the trip.
2. Find a substitute teacher.
3. Notify other teachers of the team's absence.
4. Write out a detailed itinerary of the trip.

Finally, let's prioritize (according to urgency) the items under "Optional."

It takes two weeks to receive new uniforms, so they must be ordered immediately. It will also take time to locate and retrieve game tapes so someone needs to get started on that right away. The extra practices need to be scheduled quickly so everyone involved can rearrange their schedule. Tickets to the amusement park could probably be purchased at the gate.

So the same list, prioritized according to urgency, would look like this:

1. Buy new uniforms.
2. Get game films of the competing teams.
3. Schedule several extra practices.
4. Make arrangements to visit the amusement park.

On page 134 I said that scheduling should be based on priority, economy of time and effort, and logical progression. We've just discussed priority, now let's talk about economy of time and effort.

Economy of Time and Effort

After all tasks have been prioritized according to importance and urgency, the next question to ask, before we begin scheduling, is: "Can I save time and effort by grouping several tasks together, regardless of their relative priority?" If the answer is yes, it's usually advantageous to do so. For instance, a businessman living in Dallas may need to visit three of his clients, two of which are in Chicago and one is in New York. One of the clients in Chicago represents his largest account but the other Chicago account is small. The New York account is his second largest. If he planned his trip based solely on priority, he would have to go to Chicago first to take care of his largest account, then make the trip to New York for his second visit, and then commute back to Chicago for the small client. Obviously, that wouldn't be the sensible thing to do. When we're scheduling various tasks, in addition to priority, we should consider economy of time and effort; can I pool several tasks together to be more efficient?

Concerning the basketball tournament, there are several tasks that should be combined to save time and effort. Lumping several tasks together may take them out of priority but the time and effort you'll save will justify the transition. If we look back at the lists which are arranged by priority, we'll notice that there are several times that we need to communicate to the parents of the players.

Contact the parents to see who can participate.

Get permission slips from the parents.

Solicit sponsors for the trip.

Apprise the parents of extra practices.

This list has items from all three categories: most important, important, but not critical, and optional. But it just makes good sense to do all four tasks at once. Write one, thorough memorandum to the parents, telling them about the trip, the schedule for extra practices, the need for some volunteer sponsors, and if their child is to go on the trip, they'll need to complete the parent's permission form on the back of the memorandum. As part of the parent's permission form, you might even request the correct uniform size of their child so you'll know what sizes of uniforms to order for the team.

There are other tasks that could be combined. When you call for reservations, ask the hotels to send you information about the amusement park. And while you are on the telephone, call the tournament organizer and tell him you're coming!

If you'll consider the economy of time and effort factor when scheduling your day, your daily productivity will sharply increase. Glance down your catch-all list and see how many things can be grouped together because they share a common element. For instance, make all the phone calls you need to make at one time. When you're running errands around town, plan your trip so you can include several different stops in one outing. Before you talk to someone, make a list of everything you need to talk about so you don't have to keep calling back. When you're scheduling, consider time and effort.

But there's one more thing to consider before we begin scheduling: logical progression.

Logical Progression

When we consider logical progression we simply ask the question, "Are certain tasks dependent on the completion of other tasks, and if so, what is the logical sequence?" If you fail to consider logical progression, the results can be embarrassing as well as ineffective. Buying a car before your loan is approved is a breach of logical progression. As is mopping the floor before you sweep it. Quite often we shoot ourselves in the foot because we make a decision before we get permission. I've heard it said, "It's easier to ask forgiveness than permission" but that mode of operation will get you in trouble.

Relative to our basketball tournament, there are obviously several tasks that must be done in sequence. If you make hotel reservations before you talk to the principal about whether or not you can go, you may have to make another, embarrassing call to the hotel if your principal says no. You would not send the all-inclusive memorandum to the parents before you were sure the trip was approved by the principal. And you really can't inform your fellow teachers about which students are going to miss school for a week until you find out exactly who's going on the trip.

Logical progression is usually fairly easy to determine; we just need to consider it.

So the third step in effective scheduling is to schedule based on three things: priority (importance and urgency), economy of time and effort, and logical progression. It's like looking at an object through three different lenses. Each lens shows a different aspect and brings into focus different variables. The general rule is: *Always schedule based on priorities, unless the economy of time and effort and logical progression factors are violated. If they are, adjust the schedule accordingly.*

4. Control the use of your datebook by dividing it into three parts: (a) nondiscretionary time, (b) to-do list, (c) daily report section.

Nondiscretionary Time

There are times during each day that you have little, if any, control over your schedule. If you have a weekly staff meeting every Monday from 4:00 – 5:00 P.M., that is nondiscretionary time. If your softball team practices every Friday night at 7:00 P.M., that's time that you have little control over. If you're having lunch with a business associate next Wednesday, that's a part of your day that you've already committed to.

Some jobs allow for little, if any, discretionary time during the day. A secretary who works in a busy office probably doesn't have any time during the day in which she is free to schedule according to her own desires; her schedule is predetermined from 9:00 to 5:00. Even a physician has very little control over his daily schedule because his appointments are set weeks in advance. Likewise, a school teacher is usually committed to a strict regimen of classes and staff meetings.

However, there are some jobs that allow great flexibility in the daily schedule. Most sales reps have a great deal of control over their daily schedules. Except for an occasional sales meeting, most of their time is discretionary. Managers and business executives also usually have a degree of control over their daily schedules. That's not to say that these professionals are not busy, it's just that they have more control of their time.

The first thing that should be entered in your datebook is your nondiscretionary time. Even if you're in a profession that allows you great flexibility, as soon as you make a commitment, even if it's a one-time appointment, enter it in your datebook. In the Day-Timer system there's a place on each daily ledger titled "Appointments, Scheduled Events." That's where you list nondiscretionary commitments. On page 146 is a sample Day-Timer page with only nondiscretionary items filled for March 28.

To-do List

You'll notice that on the Day-Timer page, to the left of where we put nondiscretionary events, there is a section titled "To Be Done Today." This is where you list tasks that you want to do during your *discretionary* time. These are simply things you want to get done during the day. Where do these tasks come from? From your plans and goals sheets, your catch-all list, and your project worksheets. At the beginning of each day, or better yet, the night before, check all three sources and schedule tasks based on priority, economy of time and effort, and logical progression. If you have a lot of discretionary time during the day, you may have ten tasks on your "to-do list." If

TUESDAY • March 29, 1988   89th Day, 277 Days Left • 13th Week

To be done today (number each item)	Appointments, scheduled events	hours	Diary, services performed, expenses	$	time
		8			
		9			
		10			
		11			
		12			
		1			
		2			
		3			
		4			
		5			
		6			

WEDNESDAY • March 30, 1988   90th Day, 276 Days Left

To be done today (number each item)	Appointments, scheduled events	hours	Diary, services performed, expenses	$	time
		8			
		9			
		10			
		11			
		12			
		1			
		2			
		3			
		4			
		5			
		6			

you're booked solid the entire day, you may only have five items.

Now refer back to the Day-Timer sheet on page 147. You'll notice that on March 29, 1988, both the nondiscretionary area and the to-do list are filled in. I've also placed an asterisk next to several entries on the to-do list. This is my way of labeling urgent matters, things that must be done that day. The asterisk gets my attention.

Daily Report Section

The third part of the daily ledger provides room to write notes about things that happen during the day. I call it the daily report section, on the Day-Timer page it's called "Diary, Services Performed, Expenses." If you write small, it's amazing how much information you can record in that little space. It may be hard to get out of the habit of writing notes on pieces of paper scattered all over your desk, but if you'll keep your datebook available and open during the day, you'll find it handy to transcribe all pertinent information directly onto the appropriate day's space. This becomes your daily diary. In this space don't list things you *want* to do, record things that *happened.*

If a friend calls to tell you that he's getting married, write all the information about the wedding in the daily report section. If you're out shopping for a refrigerator, write down the model number and price of the units you look at. When a client calls and places an order, even if the order is too involved to record in the space available, at least write down who called and the essence of your conversation.

If you stick with the system, the daily report section will become an invaluable record of all pertinent data. You can also use it to cross-reference information and validate transactions. Instead of throwing away your datebook at the end of each year (or each month, depending on which system you use), you'll want to keep it on file because it contains a detailed record of your daily life.

On the Day-Timer example sheet, March 30 has all three categories filled in.

Don't use your datebook as a scratch pad or as a place to record random information; control the use of your datebook by restricting use to these three areas: nondiscretionary time, to-do list, and daily report section.

5. Commit yourself to a consistent scheduling cycle.

Schedule monthly—consider long-range goals.
Schedule weekly—consider medium-range goals.
Schedule daily—consider short-range goals.

Scheduling must be done on a daily basis. You may prefer to allocate some time early in the morning, or you may want to do your scheduling the night before. It doesn't take a lot of time, usually five or ten minutes will suffice. Those few minutes invested in scheduling your upcoming day will pay great dividends. If we schedule daily, we'll be able to manage both urgent matters and day-to-day activities necessary to maintain an orderly and efficient lifestyle, such as grocery shopping, doing the laundry, paying bills, and servicing the car.

But if you only schedule daily, you'll quickly lose sight of the big picture. You'll remain so close to the demands of the moment that you'll neglect more important items. That's why you need to consider your schedule on a weekly and monthly basis. In addition to scheduling daily, choose a time once a week, perhaps on Sunday evening, when you can anticipate the entire next week. This is a particularly good time to plan your nondiscretionary time such as appointments and meetings. Also consider what you want to do each evening. Remember, your scheduling shouldn't stop when you leave work.

Follow the same procedure on a monthly basis. Select a day of the month, perhaps the last day of every month, and devote about thirty minutes to scheduling major events for the next month. For instance, consider what you want to do on each weekend. Also, look through your plans and goals, monitor your progress, and then schedule some tasks that will produce some solid gains toward accomplishing them. And while you're doing monthly planning, project on into the future; perhaps consider the next six to nine months. This is when you'll consider items like vacation time, major emphases, and broad directions.

Making a commitment to a regular, consistent scheduling cycle will produce productive days, weeks, and months. It will also help you accomplish your goals.

Scheduling should be considered the *"sine qua non"* (without which nothing) of strategic living. It is that important. If you'll incorporate these five elements of scheduling into your lifestyle, you'll notice a significant and lasting improvement in your ability to accomplish your life's goals.

Discussion Questions

1. Do you currently use a calendar book? If so, is it adequate for all your scheduling needs?
2. When would be the best time for you to do daily, weekly, and monthly scheduling?
3. Which projects are you working on that need to be written out on a project worksheet?
4. Take one of the short-range goals you have reduced into small units of work and prioritize all the component parts according to importance and urgency.

5. Now take the same goal you used in question 4 and consider the economy of time and effort and logical progression factors.
6. Make a list of all the urgent things you need to do this week.

7

Excuse Me, I'm Busy
Becoming Efficient

T here's a significant difference between effectiveness and efficiency. Effectiveness pertains to *what* we do and efficiency has to do with *how* we do it. We are effective when we do the right thing; we are efficient when we do the right thing in the most advantageous manner. For instance, when you're going on a trip, to be effective you need to correctly identify your final destination and eventually get there. To be efficient, you need to consider the best way to get there.

Obviously, it's more important to be effective than to be efficient. If we're only efficient, we may look good and appear productive, but in due time we realize that we have gone nowhere, or where we are is not where we wanted to be.

That's why busyness means nothing. Many people are busy all day long (and there's even a degree of organization and poise to their busyness), but their busyness does not produce any significant results. We must not confuse activity with results. Alec Mackensie, well-known

153

management consultant, underlined this fact when he said, "Nothing is easier than being busy and nothing more difficult than being effective." It's better to do one or two meaningful tasks per day than to do a multitude of non-directed activities. Or as the popular lecturer Zig Ziglar puts it, "There is no point in doing well that which you should not be doing at all." And that's what the first five chapters of this book have stressed: know where you want to go and then schedule smaller tasks which will help you achieve the larger goals.

Effectiveness *is* more important than efficiency, but happy and productive is the person who has both! If you have to concentrate on one, choose to be effective. But once you have become effective, work on being efficient. It's not that we have to choose one or the other—it's a matter of priority.

In this chapter, we're going to talk about becoming efficient. I'm assuming that you've worked through the goal-setting process and you know what you want to do. Now, let's discuss how you can do what you want to do in the most productive manner. Let's talk about efficiency.

Concentrate on Load-Bearing Tasks

Vilfredo Pareto, a mathematician, sociologist, and economist of the 1800s, laid the groundwork for what has become the 80/20 rule. Pareto theorized that in any given group there are relatively few "significant" items, and that attention must be placed on these if maximum results are to be expected. Stated another way, 80 percent of the results will come from 20 percent of the events. For instance, an insurance company discovered that 80 percent of its income came from 20 percent of its clients. A manufacturing firm realized that 80 percent of its sales was coming from 20 percent of its product line.

In most churches 20 percent of the people do 80 percent of the work and give 80 percent of the income.

This theory should have tremendous impact on our approach to scheduling and prioritizing. We must realize that of all the projects we could be working on, 20 percent of them will produce 80 percent of the results. The challenge is to identify that 20 percent and do it first. That's prioritizing!

Fifty years ago, Ivy Lee approached Charles Schwab, president of Bethlehem Steel, and made him a proposition. Ivy would share with Charles a simple plan for effective prioritizing and time-management, and, if the plan worked, Charles would pay him what Charles thought it was worth. The plan was: At the beginning of each day, make a list of what you need to do *in order of importance.* Begin your day by working on item Number 1 and stay with it until you finish the task, or until you can't progress any further. Then go to item Number 2 and do the same, and continue through your list. Begin each day with a new list.

Charles put the suggestion into practice and asked his managers to follow suit. The results were so beneficial that Charles sent Ivy a check for $25,000—a handsome payment during the 1930s!

Learn to Use Small Units of Time

Our days are filled with small units of time which, because of their isolation, are usually wasted. We may wait ten minutes for a friend to return a phone call, fifteen minutes for a meeting to begin, twelve minutes for the school bell to ring, twenty minutes in the cafeteria line, or five minutes at the service station. Combined, these small units can make a serious dent in an otherwise productive day.

Once you spot them, there are many projects that fit

nicely into these small cubicles of time. You can: prepare
a shopping list, write a letter, return a phone call, man-
icure your nails, plan the following day's activities, read—
the list is endless. Several weeks ago I wanted to dem-
onstrate to my wife that I was a patient, selfless, loving
husband, so I went shopping with her. For half-a-day I
felt like a dog on a leash, following my wife from store to
store. There's not much to do in a ladies' dress shop while
your wife is trying on clothes, and I soon realized that I
was wasting some valuable, though disjointed, time. Rebuked by self, I reached for my pen and notepad which I
always carry in my pocket, and in the course of visiting
two more shops, I had written the outline for a new article.

Eliminate Time Wasters

Once you have scheduled your day, you then have to
defend your schedule. Time wasters, like termites, take
small bites but the accumulative effect can be devastat-
ing. It takes effort to eradicate these pests.

Eliminate Interruptions

We all need a little flexibility built into our schedules
but, by and large, we allow too many interruptions to
sidetrack our daily progress. The number, impact, and
duration of interruptions should be controlled. Here are
a few suggestions:

Have someone else intercept your telephone calls. A sec-
    retary or family member can usually receive your
    calls, take a message, and in many cases, handle the
    need.

Schedule uninterrupted time and let everybody know that this time is inviolate for any reason short of an emergency.

Avoid being interrupted by "urgent" matters. There is a constant conflict between what is important and what is urgent. They are seldom the same. If we're not careful, we'll allow urgent tasks, which call for instant action, to distract us from important tasks. Granted, there are situations that demand immediate response: if the kitchen catches on fire—put it out! However most urgent calls can wait. Just ask yourself, "What would happen if I weren't even here?"

Learn key phrases that will help you avoid interruptions or at least shorten the interruptions. Phrases like: "I'm working on something else right now; can we talk about this later?" "I would like to visit with you about that; let's set a time to meet." "Could it wait until tomorrow; I'm really busy right now." "I've got about five minutes—is that long enough?" "Let's talk about that at staff meeting."

Work Expeditiously

Don't allow any task to take longer than it should. For instance:

Identify long-winded people and correspond with them via written memo.

Talk to people in their setting instead of letting them come into yours. (It's easier to excuse yourself than to have to excuse them.)

Get right to the point in meetings, conversations, and correspondence. Then be succinct, and when the issue is settled, go to something else.

Establish short-term deadlines for daily work. Give
yourself one hour to write that report, and then try
your best to stay within the deadline. If successful,
reward yourself with a cup of coffee, and then start
the clock on another project. Self-imposed deadlines
will help overcome indecision, interruptions, and
procrastination.

Guard against the negative aspect of perfectionism. A
perfectionist will often spend an unnecessary amount
of time on a project, not wanting to stop until every
detail is perfect. You can spend thirty minutes or two
hours washing your car. The thirty-minute job will
usually suffice. Furthermore, there are "perfect" jobs
that never get done or get done too late because they
are continually reworked. Every project has a point
of diminishing return. Learn where to draw the line
so you won't invest an inordinate amount of time
and effort with little benefit in return.

Learn to Focus

Occasionally we amaze ourselves at how much we're
able to produce when, remembering an impending deadline for a certain project, we pour ourselves into the project and stay with it until it's finished. Focused energy
always has more impact than dispersed energy. Emerson
put it this way, "As the gardener, by severe pruning, forces
the sap of the tree into one or two vigorous limbs, so
should you stop off your miscellaneous activity and concentrate your force on one or a few points." Put in more
tangible terms, there is a considerable difference between
a tennis shoe-clad, 120-pound person stepping on your toe,
and a 120-pound woman stepping on your toe with the
heel of her high-heel shoe. The weight is the same but
the pain level produced is not. We should approach every

project with focus and concentration, not just those with an imminent deadline or those of a crisis nature.

Consolidate

Much of our time and energy is wasted on unnecessary and extraneous effort because we don't consolidate our work. Leon Tec tells an anecdote which humorously illustrates this waste of energy.

Do you know the old joke about the three men who come into a grocery store together? One of them asks for a pound of nuts, obliging the clerk to get a ladder, climb to a top shelf, get the can, come down the ladder, measure out the nuts, climb back up the ladder, put the can back, come down the ladder. After he's done all this he turns to the next man. The second man also asks for a pound of nuts. This time the clerk is clever. Instead of climbing up to get the nuts, he asks the third man, "And what about you? Do you want a pound of nuts, too?"

"No," the man says.

So the clerk climbs up, gets the nuts, climbs down, measures them, and returns them. When he's finished he turns to the third man, who says, "I'd just like a *half* a pound of nuts!"

Learn to group similar tasks and do them at one time. Pay all your bills once a month, at one sitting. Return phone messages twice a day. Dictate letters to your secretary all at one time. If you're going shopping, make a list of everything you can do while you're out; don't make trips for single items. You can even consolidate space in order to be more efficient. Arrange your work station to where you have easy access to files, reports, computer terminals, reference books, pencils, and so forth.

Consolidation helps eliminate dead time, which is created by skipping from one project to another. Also, we can work faster when doing similar tasks because our minds get "on track."

Learn to Say "No"

This simple, two-letter word can be the best time management tool you'll ever acquire. Learn how to say it tactfully and graciously but learn how to say it! Our time, in the hands of others, is governed by the "sponge" effect; the bigger sponge you throw out, the more you'll soak up. It's possible to lose significant control over your life because you can't pronounce that two-letter word at the appropriate time. I once suffered from the "can't say no" syndrome. My wife, in jest (I think), made me repeat that word over and over again every evening, so it would flow more freely from my lips the next day at the office. I discovered it's rather painless, and you don't even lose any friends.

Edwin Bliss, time-management expert, says this about learning to say *no:*

> We all want to contribute to society and to our organizations and our families; most of us are happy to do our fair share. But when, because of timidity or misplaced altruism, we accept responsibilities that are too burdensome, we are being unfair to our family, our associates, our organization, and ourselves. Some groups and some people are insensitive and insatiable in their demands. To overcommit your time in such circumstances should be thought of as weakness, not willingness.

Eliminate Indecision and Cumbersome Decision-Making Processes

Indecision can paralyze progress. A ponderous decision-making policy can do the same. H. Ross Perot, president of E.D.S., compared the decision-making process of his company to more methodical companies when he said, "Around E.D.S., if anyone sees a snake, they step on it and kill it. In other companies they form a committee, collect data, research the problem, and wait until they have a consensus of opinion before they act."

A cumbersome decision-making process can easily be remedied by centralizing and clarifying decision-making authority. It's much easier if one person is responsible, be it a large corporation or your eighth-grader's graduation party.

Sometimes any decision is better than none, and the best decision, if made too late, is obviously of no value. Granted, in the case of a major decision, ample time should be allowed so all the facts can be considered. If you're considering a career change, take your time; if your boyfriend of six months just asked you to marry him, don't be in a hurry to make a decision. But typical day-to-day decisions should be resolved quickly. It probably will not matter whether you eat Mexican or Italian food for lunch, if you schedule the party for Monday or Tuesday night, or if you paint the doghouse white or gray. Don't get bogged down by decisions which don't matter that much. Some people spend more time deciding on a pet than they do their profession. Let the time spent in decision making be regulated by the importance of the decision.

Indecision has only one cure—*decide!* Often there will be a marginal difference between the outcome of two alternatives—certainly not enough to warrant the ills of indecision. Besides, if you decide quickly and make the wrong choice, you'll have more time to correct your mistake.

Clarify what decision needs to be made, who is going to make it, the deadline for the decision, and then do it! Decisiveness will help make you efficient.

Get Organized

What do we mean when we say, "Bob is an organized person"? We readily agree that organization is the friend of efficiency but what does "being organized" entail? What is it about Bob that we would be willing to grant him the merit badge of organization?

My first thought is, Bob's a good *planner*. He not only plans in order to be effective but he also plans in order to be efficient. He realizes that a high level of productivity cannot be sustained without a continuous commitment to planning. He's future-oriented; he's not always hustling to do something at the last minute because he works with a good lead time on all projects. You even suspect that if you looked at his schedule book for next week, it would already be half-filled.

Bob also has *proficient access* to all pertinent goods. He can retrieve anything he needs in a short period of time. If he needs a crescent wrench to fix the lawn mower, he knows right where it is. His filing system is more than adequate; he doesn't panic when the I. R. S. calls him for an audit. He may, depending upon style, appear to be very neat although it's possible to be organized and not appear orderly (consider the frenzied activity and cluttered environment of the New York Stock Exchange but realize the extreme degree of organization involved).

Bob also appears to be in *control*. He's in control of his time, money, possessions, even the bushes in front of his house are all cut to the same height. It's not that he has a vise grip on his resources; he just manages well. He doesn't get overcommitted nor does he try to function in an area which he knows nothing about, because then he would be out of control and would appear disorganized. Yes, Bob is organized and that helps him be efficient.

You have to work at being efficient. It's not a hereditary trait and can't be purchased in the marketplace. It takes conscientious effort over a long period of time to fine-tune the process. To learn more quickly, you might try the apprenticeship method. Identify the most efficient people you know and study them for a while. Observe how they get things done, and then make adjustments to fit your own mode of operations. Remember—effectiveness is doing the right things; efficiency is doing things right. Cultivate both!

Discussion Questions

1. On a scale of 1 to 10 rate yourself in terms of being efficient. Substantiate your opinion.
2. What are your priorities in life? Prioritize the fourteen six-month goals you developed at the end of the previous chapter.
3. List ten projects that you need to do that can be done in less than ten minutes. Complete all ten items in the next two days using small units of time that would otherwise be wasted.
4. Identify the major "time wasters" in your life. How can you eliminate them?
5. Do you have a hard time saying "no"? If so, why?
6. List all the decisions you need to make but haven't. Analyze the reason for your indecision and then set a deadline for each decision.

8

To Run the Race
Zeal and Sacrifice

wenty-six miles, 385 yards, is a long way to run. Emil Zatopek, after winning the Olympic marathon gold medal in 1952, said, "If you want to run, then run a mile. If you want to experience another life, run a marathon." The hollow-eyed, gaunt stare of a runner in the twenty-sixth mile is evidence enough that the marathon is perhaps the ultimate in athletic endurance. In most races, the winner is defined as the one who crosses the finish line first; in a marathon, everyone who finishes the race is a winner.

A Physical Goal

My wife and I traditionally reserve the week between Christmas and New Year's for our yearly planning. The holiday season usually provides a lull in our fast pace, and the end of the year is an appropriate time to reflect back on the previous twelve months and to look ahead to the future. I firmly believe that plans and goals must be written down if they're to be fully effective, so we emerge from the week with several pages of plans we want to accomplish in the upcoming year. We usually have four or five items under each of the main categories previously discussed in chapter 4 (SPIRITUAL, PERSONAL, FAMILY, PHYSICAL, and so forth). In December 1984, I placed an unusual entry under PHYSICAL goals: *Run the New York Marathon*. It was unusual because I'm not a runner. Heretofore my witty response to the thought of running was, "The day I see a smiling jogger is the day I may consider becoming a participant." I had never run a race and had not participated in any form of consistent exercise in five years.

On October 27, 1985, at 3:40 in the afternoon, I passed under a large banner in Central Park which read: "FINISH-NEW YORK CITY MARATHON." The race was the culmination of eight months of strenuous training and was the fulfillment of a formidable challenge.

I'm still not sure why I wanted to run a marathon. I remember thinking that I had set and accomplished many spiritual, educational, and intellectual goals, but I had never accepted a difficult physical challenge. In retrospect, God placed in my heart the desire to run a marathon for reasons which only became apparent during the course of training and during the race itself. The entire endeavor provided a laboratory environment in which I could experientially learn certain truths, which otherwise would be hard to learn. For instance, I learned that . . .

We can achieve great things if we'll just try.

Great accomplishments are not out of the reach of most men and women. The problem is we just don't try. When was the last time you attempted the unusual—

something which was a departure from your comfort zone? For me, a marathon was so far out of my comfort zone, it was in the twilight zone! My training book suggested that a runner should not attempt a marathon unless he had been running for at least two years. Eight months before the marathon, my first day on the track, I couldn't run a mile without stopping. And yet, eight months later, I was one of fifteen thousand who crossed the finish line.

The Success Syndrome

Partly to blame for our timidity and lack of initiative in accepting challenging goals is the success syndrome that has become endemic to our American culture. We're shackled by a "Number One" mentality; the person who comes in "Number One" is the only one worthy of recognition. Do we realize the futility of this mind set? In any given situation, there can be only one "Number One." That means everyone else is subpar—each failed. In a mile race, the "winner's" time is 04.32, the next guy finishes in 04.33. Does that make him a failure? Of course not. I like the U.S. Army's slogan "Be All That You Can Be." Often we hesitate to attempt great things because we're not sure if we will be "the best." Forget the best— be the best *you* can be.

The fear of failure is a similar threat to our interest in accomplishment. We're so paranoid about failure that we abort projects upon the first sign of potential problems. Success is not the absence of failure; success is the progressive realization of worthwhile goals, and failure is usually a necessary step to success. Babe Ruth struck out 1,330 times in his career but he's remembered for his 714 career home runs and his lifetime-batting average of .342. For the great left-handed slugger, striking out was just the downside of hitting home runs.

There's always risk involved when we pursue an opportunity or take initiative in a new area, but along with speculation comes the chance of great reward. It has even been suggested that part of the entrepreneurial spirit of our country is due to the fact that all those who left their home country to come to America were risk takers. Those who embraced security and comfort stayed at home.

We've often heard the proverb, "If it's worth doing, it's worth doing right." I prefer another version, "If it's worth doing, it's worth doing wrong, at least at the beginning, because anything worth doing is going to be difficult, and perfection will only come through repeated failure." I'm glad we didn't quit trying to walk because we repeatedly stumbled at the onset. Consider failure as a stepping-stone to success, not a roadblock—just a means to an end. If the fear of failure motivates us to hard work, efficiency, and conscientiousness—fine! If it restrains us from attempting great things—reject it.

Even a small dose of naiveté is often to one's advantage. Many times in my life, I set out to accomplish something big when, halfway through the project, I thought: "If I had known it was going to be this involved and this difficult, I would never have tried." Without exception, the project was completed and proved to be worth all the stretching that was required.

What are the things you've always dreamed of doing, but for one reason or another the projects remain in dreamland? Such ventures as: finishing a graduate degree, starting a business, touring the world, running for political office, writing a book? Get God's approval and go for it! Running a marathon was a drastic departure from my norm, and halfway through my training schedule, I thought, "What in the world have I gotten myself into?"

However, I finished the race, and it was worth the cost.

I not only discovered that we can achieve great things if we will simply try but I quickly realized that . . .

A workable strategy must be developed for every goal.

Being a novice at the sport of running, I needed to gain some knowledge to go along with my zeal, so I made a trip to my favorite bookstore and bought four books on running. I soon learned all about running shoes, special diet, the history of the marathon, training schedules, current records, speed-distance-and-hill training, dealing with injuries, and many other areas that concern runners. The most valuable discovery of my reading was an eight-month training schedule designed by one of the authors. The schedule indicated the number of miles which should be run every day for eight months prior to the race. During the first week, twenty-five miles of running was required, and the total mileage for each subsequent week gradually increased until it reached fifty miles per week for the five weeks before the race. The author indicated that if a runner used this training schedule, he would finish the marathon, and do so in a respectable time and fashion. This training chart became the crux of my strategy.

Learn from the Veterans (Not the Researchers)

Every goal must be accompanied by a strategy. Deciding *what* you want to do produces a *goal;* determining *how* to do it produces a *strategy*. Many worthwhile goals experience a quick death or perpetual convalescence because a plausible and complete strategy is never developed. A goal without a strategy is like a record without a turntable. Great potential is available but it remains dormant until it's activated.

To develop a legitimate strategy, consult those who have already been successful at what you're planning to do. If your goal is to lose forty pounds, visit with several people who have already lost weight. If you want to swim the English Channel, talk with those who have. If you want to earn a medical degree, consult with some doctors who have just graduated. Be sure to confer with those who have actually done it—those who have first-hand experiential success. It's surprising how many "experts" there are in every field who have no idea what they're talking about because they've been observers or researchers but *not* participants.

You can also learn the strategy of veterans by reading their books. I have yet to enjoy a private conversation with a world-class runner, but I have gleaned what they have to offer because I read their books. The challenge here is that there are so many books written on every subject, it's often difficult to wade through the mediocre and select the "classics."

A properly developed strategy will reveal several important things. First, it will tell you the cost which you'll have to pay to achieve your goal. The mere statement of a goal usually doesn't clearly define the price tag, but a detailed strategy will let you know the cost of the endeavor, which enables you to weigh the cost against the benefit to be derived. You may realize that it's not worth the cost. Furthermore, a thorough strategy will allow you to assess whether or not the goal is feasible—that is, is it possible for you to do?

I once had the wild thought of swimming the English Channel. It sounded like an exciting goal to achieve. However, when I investigated the matter more closely, the goal was aborted because the cost was too great (a minimum of three to four training hours per day), and I didn't possess the talent and skill to finish the goal (one must be an excellent swimmer).

A goal which captures the imagination coupled with a sound strategy is a dynamic combination. My goal was to run a marathon, and I designed a training strategy based on the recommendations of several professionals. Halfway through the eight months of training, I realized that another element was necessary . . .

Strategy must be executed with determination and tenacity.

Worthwhile goals are always difficult to achieve. If they weren't, everyone would participate. Once a goal is set, and a strategy is designed, the difference between success and failure is usually decided by the presence or absence of one character trait—determination. During the course of achieving a goal, inspiration will wane, excitement will come and go, desire will often decline, resources may become scant, and even outside forces may resist progress. At this point, determination must be available and activated.

The Determination Factor

In my training for the race, determination was a key factor. There were times when maintaining the schedule required running from 11:00 P.M. into the morning hours. At other times, it required running in torrential rain or excessive heat. I kept wondering when it was going to become fun (it never did). The first time I ran twelve miles, I felt so miserable I questioned the validity of the entire project. At those moments, the determination factor was the only thing that sustained the program.

There is a fine degree of distinction between stubbornness and determination. They are both made of the same substance; the difference is in application. Determination and stubbornness are both willing to pay whatever cost is necessary to complete a project, and they're willing to confront and deal with problems and resistance encountered along the way. When this willingness is channeled toward a meaningful, God-given goal, it's called *determination;* when it's focused on selfish and unreasonable goals, it's called *stubbornness.*

Determination is a human character trait. A program does not have determination; a person does, and it's not a commodity you buy at the store. It must be developed. When the circumstances of life demand determination, at that point it's either spawned or disregarded. We acquire determination by responding favorably to situations that demand it. Once it's a part of our character, it can be summoned and utilized whenever needed.

Determination is a must in any large endeavor. Often the prize is not given to the most skillful or the wisest or the most capable, it's awarded to the one who has determination.

During the course of training for the race, another "law" influencing the accomplishment of goals became very important . . .

In mature planning, there must be proper respect given to foundation building.

In running it's simply called: *building foundation miles.* A runner must develop a large quantity of training miles in order to provide a base from which race miles are run. It would be ridiculous to think that one could run six miles without any training. Likewise, it would be foolish to attempt a 15-mile run if the daily average was only 2.

My schedule built from a base of 25 miles per week and climaxed at 50 miles per week, several weeks before the race. The last month I logged nearly 200 miles, an adequate foundation from which to attempt 26.2.

The Foundation Factor

This concept is so obvious you might be inclined to echo the words of Sherlock Holmes, "That's elementary." But in teaching planning seminars, I often consult individuals who think they can skip the foundation aspect—but it can't be done. For instance, some people may decide to start memorizing Scripture, so they set a goal of five verses per week. Within a month, they're off-schedule, frustrated, and defeated. They end the year having memorized ten verses—the ones they memorized the first two weeks. I suggest that they reduce their lofty ambitions and begin to memorize just one verse a week or even two per month. Maintain this level for two years, then attempt two per week. In the fourth year, the goal of five verses memorized per week will be feasible *because a foundation has been laid.*

Similarly, if you want to have a savings account, to begin with, target no more than 5 percent of your annual salary. If you've never disciplined yourself to save, don't think you can begin with 10 percent or more—it won't work. Likewise, if you decide to start reading regularly, set your first year goal at one book per month; a more challenging goal will lead to undue stress, frustration, and defeat.

A commitment to foundation building will protect us from the "get it quick" mentality which pervades our society. Items of worth, whether tangible or intangible, are best acquired slowly. Foundation building will help us avoid the temptation of getting something for nothing, rising to the top too quickly, taking shortcuts, and all the headaches that accompany such foolishness. Instead, we will commit ourselves to steady, solid growth, based on a firm foundation.

When our toddlers become mobile, they progress through a very systematic routine: *crawl, walk, run.* Each action must be done in order. It's futile to try to walk before you crawl, and even more ridiculous to try to run before you walk. God seems to have created us in such a fashion that foundation building is a must. A tree never grows beyond what its roots can support. Why do we try to extend ourselves beyond the support of our foundation?

A commitment to a goal should bring with it a commitment to build a foundation. Whenever we set a goal we must ask, "Do I have the necessary foundation to achieve this goal?" The answer may be *yes,* but if it's *no,* then we must ask, "Am I willing to pay the price (time, energy, tangible resources) to build a foundation?"

While training for the race, I also noticed an unusual amount of inertia being developed and utilized, and I discovered that . . .

Goals motivate—they serve as the catalyst for dormant resources.

For years prior to the marathon experience, I had tried many times to be consistent in the area of physical exercise. One year I would try to run several days a week. (That would last about five weeks.) The next year I would purchase a membership in a health club and schedule to work out three days a week. That great aspiration would also soon fade. Next came a convenient ten-minute exercise plan which could be done every evening at home. That plan soon met a similar demise. The problem was I had no concrete goal to aim at. My motivation for wanting to exercise was too broad and lacked accountability. I simply wanted to "stay in shape." But once I confirmed the goal of running a marathon, I began to experience discipline, tenacity, and control to a degree that was heretofore untapped.

The Goal Factor

In any given situation there are masses of resources which are unused or misused because they are misdirected. A goal will activate these resources and channel them in a unified direction. A God-inspired goal will also be a catalyst for faith. Just as faith is the substance of things unseen, a goal is a vision of things unseen. They are related. If you are confident that God has directed you toward a certain goal, the immeasurable momentum of faith will soon be rolling your way.

But in order for goals to motivate, it is a good practice to . . .

Make your goals public and solicit help toward achieving your goal.

The chances of success greatly increase when you go public with your intentions. I let this marathon idea simmer in my mind for a few months, and when I decided to go for it, I told all my friends and work associates. Boy, were they impressed! My pastor even announced from the pulpit on Sunday that I was going to run a marathon. From that point on, there was no turning back. Call it pride if you want, but once the word was out; my ego was on the line, and I was determined to finish the race. Going public with your goals produces a healthy pressure which will motivate you to achieve.

Comrades on the Course

But that's not the only reason to publicize a goal. Once your aspirations have been vocalized, other people who have similar interests and goals will be attracted by your statement. Soon you will experience that wonderful sense of comaraderie that only comes when people are working toward a similar goal.

It's a lot easier to finish a fifteen-mile run when you're with someone, than when you're running alone. If for no other reason, misery enjoys company. After the big announcement was made, two young people in the church, Julee and Dwayne, emerged as my helpmates. I didn't know it, but Julee had been a competitive long-distance runner in high school and Dwayne had similar interest in developing athletic endurance. At least twice a week, we would meet at the track to run together. For long runs of more than ten miles, Dwayne would follow along on his bike with a ready supply of bananas and water. In retrospect, I don't think I could have made it without the help of those two friends. Their help and encouragement often gave me the second wind needed to endure the rigors of training. So in pursuing goals, relate to other people who have similar goals.

Also, the day of the race, I had hundreds of friends praying for me. I even felt a bit embarrassed that God would be bothered so often regarding such a mundane matter. My friends prayed and supported me because I had shared my goal with them and allowed them to help me accomplish it.

I also learned that . . .

Discipline is a character trait that must be acquired and developed.

Discipline is a character trait that must be developed. No one is "endowed" with discipline at birth, and we all start out with the same potential and necessity for developing our willpower. Our wills must be conditioned. To do this we often have to commit ourselves to tasks and schedules that don't involve things we "must do" or "want to do." For instance, if you have to be at work at 8:00 every morning, getting up at 7:00 will not necessarily develop discipline in your life because it's something you have to do in order to be on time. Try getting up at 5:30 every morning for a month—*that* will require discipline. Similarly, to claim to have a disciplined life because you eat a bowl of ice cream *every* night before you go to bed would be stretching the point (and your stomach). Try going *without* ice cream for a month—*that* will require discipline.

The Discipline Factor

Not only must discipline be acquired, it must be constantly developed or it will be lost! Discipline is like a muscle—use it or lose it. You must constantly exercise your willpower if it is to remain strong; inactivity will lead to atrophy.

Furthermore, discipline is a transferable concept. It doesn't matter in which area of life you learn discipline, once you have it as a part of your character, it can be applied to any area. Discipline can be acquired while learning a skill such as playing the piano, it may be developed through mental toughness; or it may come as a by-product of a physical regimen.

Regardless of how it's acquired, discipline is best used when applied to the pursuit of godliness. I discovered that the physical discipline acquired through training for the race could be a means to spiritual discipline. This is what Paul meant when he told young Timothy, "Discipline yourself for the purpose of godliness; for bodily discipline is only of little profit, but godliness is profitable for all things" (1 Tim. 4:7–8).

When I began training for the marathon, I thought it was only a physical pursuit. It eventually became one of the most spiritually beneficial things I've ever done. It was more advantageous to my spiritual life than a multitude of conferences, books, tapes, or sermons. Running the race gave me discipline, a missing factor in my spiritual life.

Prior to the race, my daily time with God was sporadic at best. All my good intentions were crippled by a lack of discipline. Plain and simple—I just couldn't stick with it. I would be consistent for six or seven days, then miss a few days, and soon I was out of sync and off-track.

While training for the race, I ran six days a week. Regardless of how busy my schedule was, I did find time to run—once a day, six days a week. It became the common denominator of my daily schedule. I was determined to stick with my training schedule and I didn't let anything distract me. Through the rigors of this system emerged discipline.

After the race I abandoned the daily run; I had accomplished my goal, and it was no longer necessary. But I retained the discipline factor, and transferred it to an area of my life that needed it. Physical discipline became a means to a greater end—spiritual discipline.

Another lesson I learned was that . . .

It helps to visualize the successful completion of your goal.

I knew what the finish line looked like. Grandstands on the side, the banner above which read FINISH—NEW

YORK CITY MARATHON, the large digital clock, the volunteers ready to register your running number and time,
and then wrap you in a mylar blanket and give you a
small sack of fruit and candy. I had seen it on television;
I bought books with pictures of it. I *knew* what the finish
line looked like. And during the months of training and
particularly during the race, I drew an enormous amount
of strength from visualizing what it would be like to run
past the bleachers, under the sign, past the clock, and
into the welcome service of the volunteers.

The Visualization Factor

Bill Brooks, a management consultant, tells how visualizing success helped Florence Chadwick become the
first woman to swim the English Channel.

When Florence Chadwick set out from the coast of
France to make her historic swim in 1952, she was full of
hope and courage. The lone swimmer was surrounded by
boats filled with journalists, well-wishers and a few skeptics. For years she had trained vigorously to build her
stamina and disciplined her body to keep going long after
everything within her cried out for her to quit.

As she neared the coast of England a heavy fog settled
in and the waters became increasingly cold and choppy.
"Come on Florence, you can make it!" her mother urged
as she handed her some food. "It's only a few more miles!
You're ahead of schedule!" But Florence was beaten by
the tortuous elements of nature that day.

Exhausted, she finally asked to be pulled aboard the
boat. She was heartbroken, especially when she discovered how close she'd come to her goal.

"I'm not making excuses," she later told reporters. "But
I think I could have made it if I could only have seen my
goal."

Florence determined to try again. This time, she added

a new dimension to her daily training. She studied the
shoreline of England where she expected to land, and
memorized every feature of the seacoast. Each day as she
swam, she would replay that mental image of her goal.

Eventually, she entered the waters again and set out
for the coast of England. Along the way, she ran into all
the fog, turbulence and cold water she'd met before. But
this time something was different. She swam with greater
vigor and determination. Even the skeptics noticed her
new confidence.

She became the first woman in history to swim the
English Channel.

What made the difference? She said later that it was
because she was able to keep her goal clearly in focus in
her mind, even when she couldn't see it with her eyes."

Are you struggling through medical school? Go spend
several hours in a doctor's office or in a hospital and observe the anticipated outcome of your schoolwork. Are you
having difficulty sticking with your diet? Visualize the
benefits of being trim and healthy. Has your goal of becoming more financially secure become log jammed?
Imagine what it would be like to be debt-free, or to have
a substantial savings account.

I'm currently studying violin. Sometimes it can be very
discouraging for it's a pursuit that yields very little immediate satisfaction. When I get discouraged, I play a
recording of Fritz Kreisler, or attend a symphony concert
that highlights a concert violinist. I recently asked my
instructor if he would just play for me the last five minutes of every lesson. I want to leave the lesson with his
playing in my ear—for that is the goal for which I'm
working.

In achieving goals it's also important to . . .

**Be zealous about achieving your goal and be
willing to sacrifice to attain it.**

Early Sunday morning October 30, 1983, a Mercedes truck laden with two thousand pounds of dynamite rolled past security barricades and crashed into the lobby of the headquarters of the Eighth Marine Battalion in Beirut, Lebanon. Seconds later the terrorist driver ignited the explosives and the building collapsed. Two hundred twenty-nine Marines died and eighty-one others were wounded. During a press conference that followed an investigation of the tragic incident, a reporter asked a general from the Pentagon how one man could get past such tight security and cause so much damage. The general replied: "In spite of our defensive weapons, it still is virtually impossible to stop those who are willing to die for what they believe."

The Commitment Factor

Total abandonment is a powerful force.

In training for the marathon the longest run is twenty miles. Most trainers agree that the final six should not be attempted until the race. For first-time marathoners, these are the mystery miles. Going into the race, you're just not sure what's going to happen those last six miles.

I had read stories about runners who fell into a trance during the final miles, and when the course turned left or right, they kept going straight, running into barricades, people, and buildings. Others would hit the infamous "wall" and just fall over. When my wife, who is an optimistic but cautious person, heard this, she asked me to increase my life insurance policy by $250,000 before I ran the race. That'll bless your heart!

As the day of the race drew near, a sense of abandonment developed in my heart. Three days before I left for New York I wrote some instructions on a blank 3″×5″ card, which I would later carry in the race, strapped to my waist. I covered the card with clear scotch tape so the sweat wouldn't smear the ink. I wrote:

My name is Don McMinn from Austin, Texas. I am to finish the race—do not let me stop and *do not* remove me from the course track.

DON MCMINN 10-24-85

I was determined to finish the race, and I was willing to sacrifice to do it. Fortunately, my instruction card was not needed, but I was prepared to display it to any medic who might try to interfere.

The tiny card was not a rash display of egotistical vainglory. I was just serious about finishing the race. When the starting gun sounded, I had no thought of not finishing; quitting short of the finish line was never a viable option.

I'm not saying that we need to put our life on the line every time we set a goal, but I am saying that total commitment is helpful and often necessary in order to reach certain goals. There's nothing wrong with believing in something so strongly that you're willing to sacrifice and suffer for it.

And finally, I discovered that . . .

Joy and satisfaction are the intangible rewards of accomplishing a goal.

The best definition of success I know reads like this: "Success is the progressive realization of meaningful goals." To feel successful you have to have goals, and those goals must eventually come to fruition. And when they do, you are rewarded with a wonderful sense of joy and satisfaction. And the greatest satisfaction does not come from the corollary benefits that accompany the attainment of the goal, but just from the fact that you set a goal and accomplished it.

Intangible Rewards

Suppose I had finished in first place in the race instead of 13,365th. I would have won $25,000 and a new Mercedes. But the real joy would not come from these incidental rewards but from the sheer delight of having set a goal, developed a strategy, and worked hard to achieve it.

And this, incidentally, is why we need to allow time to savor the delights of success. We need to learn how to celebrate and enjoy our accomplishments. I'm not exactly sure why God rested on the seventh day of the creation process, but I don't think it was because he was tired. I think he just wanted to enjoy what he had done. Like an artist who steps back to gaze at his painting, God took time to relish his handiwork.

When you accomplish a major goal in life, don't immediately start another one; *enjoy your accomplishment.* Take time to reflect on all that happened and glean as much as you can from your experience.

Yes, there is joy and satisfaction in strategic living. Perhaps the most satisfying words Christ ever spoke were: "It is finished." It was not a cry of defeat but a shout of victory—He had accomplished his goal in life. Paul expressed the same contentment when he said, "I have fought the good fight, I have finished the course." Paul was ready to die because he had fulfilled his purpose in living. No regrets—no second thoughts.

How about you? When you're lying on your deathbed, will you have any regrets about what you did or didn't do in life? Start setting goals for your life and then work to bring those goals to fruition.

Live strategically.

References

de Bono, Edward. *Tactics—The Art and Science of Success*. Boston: Little Brown & Co., 1984.

Engstrom, Ted W. *Motivation to Last a Lifetime*. Grand Rapids: Daybrook Books, 1984.

Gardner, John. *Excellence*. NY: Harper & Row, 1961.

Swartz, David S. *The Magic of Getting What You Want*. NY: William Morrow & Co., 1983.